MW00613451

One Voice

Janet Swanson

Second Edition

Copyright © 2014 by Janet Swanson

One Voice

By Janet Swanson

Edited by Elaine Schneider

ISBN-10: 09862275-8-7

ISBN-13: 978-0-9862275-8-5

Printed in USA

All rights reserved solely by the author. The author guarantees all contents are original and do not infringe upon the legal rights of any other person or work. No part of this book may be reproduced in any form without the permission of the author.

Table of Contents

Chapter 1: Daddy's Girl

Chapter 2: Divorce, Chaos, Confusion, Poverty

Chapter 3: Remarriage, Abuse, and Abandonment

Chapter 4: Foster Care

Chapter 5: Reuniting with my Father

Chapter 6: Looking for Love

Chapter 7: Finding Christ, Finding My Groom

Chapter 8: Heart's Desire and Heart's Loss

Chapter 9: Season of Loss

Chapter 10: Healing at Last

Dedication and Acknowledgements

I would like to dedicate this book to all the people that have been abused sexually, verbally, or physically. Abuse is abuse. And all abuse needs healing. My prayer is that in this book you will find hope in what seems to be a hopeless situation and find inner healing in the only ONE Voice, Jesus Christ!

I would like to first thank my heavenly Father for bringing me through the darkest times of my life and for giving me the joy of my salvation. Without HIM I can do nothing, or even have a reason to do so.

I would like to thank my dear sweet husband, Cary Swanson, and my three boys, Reed, Rhett, and Ryan, for being so patient with me while I finished this book. I know there were not many "home-cooked" meals in the past few months and lots of laundry that seemed to pile up way too fast! I have an awesome family and I love you all very much! Thanks for believing in me.

I would like to thank Ric Mandes for believing in me enough to write an article in the *Statesboro Magazine* about my life. The article's title – "One Voice" – struck a chord in my heart that inspired me to name the book by the same title.

I would like to thank Elaine Schneider for her love, time and support, and all the long hours she spent in editing my book. Also for her monetary gifts to help make this book happen!

I would like to thank James Lewis for his monetary gifts and for always believing in me, for speaking over me all these years and saying, "You've got what it takes" and knowing that one day I would write a book.

I would like to thank Jorge Araque for spending many long hours designing the front and back cover of this book and for always being available to help me when I called upon him.

I would like to thank all my friends and the Praise Team for always standing beside me and stepping up to the plate when I called for you! You guys are the best!

I would like to thank my brothers and sisters in Christ who have stood by me through thick and thin and have loved me unconditionally. Your love and prayers helped carry me through writing this book. I love you so much.

I would like to thank Tommy Lewis at Lewis Color for printing ONE VOICE!

Janet Swanson

Forward

Being around Janet Swanson is an adventure. Her faith is deep. Perhaps one might even say it is childlike. She believes in a God who is powerful and moves in supernatural ways. Jesus answered her cries for help from child abuse – literally – stopping the most hideous of acts just before it happened. No one else was in the room. Just Jesus. Even as a child, Janet recognized her Savior.

And Janet still believes in that God who scooped her up as a little girl and carried her through the storms and darkness of her childhood, the God who became her only light. She doesn't temper her faith with knowledge gained in adulthood or explain away things that are illogical. She calls them what they are – supernatural works of God.

Can she sing? Oh, yes. Can she speak, teach, and preach? Oh, yes. But is that all there is to Janet Swanson? Not a chance. She has a relationship with God that is unfathomable. She knows his heart and he knows hers.

During the writing of this book, I walked in a few minutes earlier than our arranged meeting time. I found Janet on her knees at the altar, not just praying, but truly worshiping. She was lost to all around her, basking in God's love and praising him for his faithfulness. Janet never even knew I was there. She was wrapped up in Jesus.

And from that faith comes the heart of this book, the revelation of a story that began in the darkest of places but was transformed into a life dedicated to serving God. Whether she is speaking or singing, Janet's voice is the reflection of her relationship to God, and the message is *his*.

Elaine Ernst Schneider

Author, Editor, Believer

Preface

My reason for this book is that you will find hope and healing in the arms of Jesus. Come and let Him heal you. May His VOICE stand out to you loud and clear as you read the pages of my life and how God brought me out of darkness into His marvelous light. What God touches never remains the same! I pray that the words of this book will jump off the page and land at the doors of your heart to draw you closer to Him.

Chapter One

Daddy's Girl

Some of my earliest and best memories were those times that it was just my daddy and me. When I was a little girl, he took me with him just about everywhere he went. I remember Daddy taking me to work with him. When he went to the beach fishing, I went to the beach fishing. When he went to the river with his boat, then I was there too.

Daddy loved the water. He had served in the Navy, so he was a great swimmer! I couldn't swim, but I wasn't afraid. I knew I was safe with my daddy. One of the greatest thrills of my childhood was when he put me on his shoulder and swam all the way across the lake at Brown's Cross Roads.

My daddy was my hero. I believed he could do anything. He constantly amazed me with his "dare-devil" antics. He was strong and brave. He could even do things like jumping into the water off high riverbanks. And he really impressed me when he climbed tall trees on the banks of the river. He would take hold of a cable anchored high up in the tree and then swing way out over the river and dive headfirst into the water. I thought my daddy was like Tarzan!

Apparently, Daddy overdid it one day. When he hit the water, there was a loud splashing sound that reminded me of the sound someone makes when they do a "belly-buster." It was like someone had slapped the water really loud. It turned out that he had pushed his luck too far. It was, in fact, more than a belly-buster; he had burst his eardrum.

I knew my daddy loved me and wanted to be with me. All the adventures we shared bonded my little heart to his. He was my hero. And I was his biggest admirer. I felt his exploits were just for me and that he loved me and wanted me to be happy. He made me feel special. I was without a doubt, "Daddy's Girl."

There was an interesting dynamic in our bond. In my world, there was no one like my daddy. In my heart, he was bigger than life itself. He knew I loved and admired him. As I look back, I remember many times when my superhero daddy asked me to pray for him. As a tiny little girl, I crawled up in bed next to him. He would open wide his arms and I snuggled up close. Then he would ask me to pray for him. And I would pray intensely. To this day, I vividly remember how strongly I felt his love for me as he tenderly embraced me. I was surely Daddy's Girl.

My daddy was a musician. He played anything that had strings on it, including the piano. And he played them all very well. He was a singer too. I imagine that because I picked up his musical talents, I may have been his most favored child because we had an incredible connection! If he didn't come home at the expected time, I would wait and wait for him until he arrived. When he walked through the door, I would run and jump into his arms, and then wrap my arms and legs around him just like a monkey. My daddy loved me and I loved my daddy.

Something's Not Right

Even as a little girl and in the certainty of my daddy's love, I began to sense something was not right in our home. I didn't know what, but I knew there was something. I began to pick up a feeling that my mother didn't love me. She didn't look at me like my daddy did. She was talented musically too. But when I sang, she didn't beam with pride like my daddy did. I yearned for her love with all my heart. I didn't feel she loved me, even though I was her little girl. This left a huge void in my life.

I grieved for my mother's love. This sense of loss – this feeling – made me cry and pray. I was too little to have such a big heartache. I remember making up sad songs. The first song I wrote was called "Nobody Loves Me and Nobody Cares." I had so much love to give, but only my daddy could see it and only he responded to it. But there were days when even my daddy didn't affirm me. Those were really bad days. It was very hard to feel that *no one* loved me at all.

My dad was a preacher, and he had a singing group. Since my mother was taught music when she was growing up, she could play the piano and sing alto. She knew how to read music. My dad just played by ear. And he was a true tenor. High notes just soared.

There was a lady in my dad's singing group who sang soprano. In fact, she was "Ms. Soprano" to me. She was captivating. She caught my daddy's eye and I guess you could say he caught hers. Daddy was a very charming man. I can remember times when my dad would compare Ms. Soprano to my mom. And because my mother smoked and never connected to people in the church, the comparison wasn't a good one. My daddy used to smoke, but he quit when he got saved; so my daddy didn't have a lot of patience with my mom's smoking habit. In fact, he really got mad at her because she wouldn't quit.

One day my mom and dad had a really bad fight. I can't remember if it had anything to do with Momma's smoking, but things heated up pretty fast. It started off with talking, then screaming, then extreme physical abuse. I was just a little girl, maybe four years old, and I saw this man that I loved so much hitting my mother. It was awful. When this had happened before, I had screamed and cried and begged him not to hit her anymore. It always broke my heart. Then when Daddy saw me crying, he would melt. I was the only one that could calm him down. My tears could stop him.

But this time, it was different. He ignored my tears. He would not stop! I remember running through the house screaming. It was a desperate situation. I decided it was up to me to stop the fight. I got a knife from the kitchen and ran into the back bedroom where my mom and dad were fighting. I screamed as loud as I could, "Daddy, stop, or I will stab you!" When he looked at me, standing there so desperate and afraid, it broke him. The fight was over.

My daddy's anger was a big problem. At times, he would get so angry that he just completely lost it. Looking back, I am sure there were a lot of things going on that a little girl simply didn't understand. When Daddy got himself into hopeless situations, he would turn to me and call me by my nickname, JJ. He would say to me, "JJ, pray for me." Then in that very moment, I would lay my little hands on him and pray. I would simply say, "In the name of Jesus, touch my daddy." Daddy knew his little girl could get to the heart of Jesus.

Divorce

I was born in Florida and lived there several years...not sure exactly how many. Believe it or not, I can actually remember living there. And I recall with some clarity that we moved around a lot. In fact, thinking back on the first six years of my life, we probably lived in six different places. That was a lot of moving!

When I was around the age of six, we lived in some sort of housing project. There was one day in particular that I remember too clearly. I woke up to see the sun shining brightly. It was a beautiful day. However, I had no idea what was going to happen that day – things that would change my life forever.

I was in the kitchen pantry with my mother. She turned to me and said the most devastating words I have ever heard in my life. Thinking of those words hurts my heart. I can still feel the pain from it. My mother said, "Your dad and I are getting a divorce and we are moving out."

Immediately, I collapsed to my knees and screamed and cried to the top of my lungs! I held nothing back. I let it all out. There was no way I could control my emotions. They were simply too strong.

I stayed in the pantry for hours, weeping and sobbing until I couldn't cry any more. I could not believe it! My daddy and my momma would no longer live under the same roof. What was going to happen to me? That bright sunny morning, my whole world turned upside down. I couldn't help but think that maybe it was my fault. My young heart had never experienced a greater pain than this. It was too much. I couldn't process it.

In one single morning, my whole life had fallen apart. With the terrible news came a major dilemma: I was faced with an incredible decision. It was a choice no child should ever have to make. How could I pick between Daddy and Momma? The relationship I had with each of them was very different; however, I had to choose with which parent I wanted to live.

Making a Choice

I loved my mom and I loved my dad. I loved them both so much! How could I choose? I had always felt my daddy loved me more than my mom did. There was no way I was going to leave my daddy! He was everything to me! I adored him. There was no one else that could even measure up to him. He was so strong. And he always protected me. He always had my back and he always loved me even in his own mess-ups. I knew that I was the apple of his eye. He especially loved to hear me sing. I could sing to him and make everything better.

And Daddy knew *me*. He knew that for a pack of M&Ms, he had me in the palm of his hand. He even kept M&Ms in his truck just in case he needed to bribe me; and if for some reason there was no "Plan B" for the M&Ms, he could give me a quarter so that I could go to the neighborhood gas station and buy myself a pack. Despite all the pain and confusion, I knew one thing for sure: My daddy loved me! How could I leave him? How could Momma leave him? What had happened?

Now, even as a grown woman, I can't put a bad light on my father. I realize that because of issues of his heart and out of his own pain, he did things he shouldn't have done.

Something had happened with Ms. Soprano in the singing group. I remember those times with her very well. There were times when she had picked me up and we had gone riding around. She could really sing. I remember harmonizing with her in the car. We liked singing, "You Light up My Life."

At this point, I have more clarity on how the divorce transpired. There's no doubt that Ms. Soprano was a major issue. However, there had been a lot of verbal and physical abuse in our home. Still, as a little six-year-old girl, I couldn't help but believe that I was the reason my mother left my dad. I just couldn't understand. Maybe there were too many females sharing my dad – my mom, Ms. Soprano, and me!

Harmony

Singing always came naturally to me. And harmony was something equally as innate. Around our house, there was a lot of harmonizing. Woe be to the one who couldn't do it! That was almost justification for being declared an outcast!

My two brothers could sing, but I never heard them harmonize at all. As a child, I didn't really understand the difference. What I did know was that singing was as natural for me as breathing. I had to breathe to sing, and singing was almost just as necessary.

On top of that, I was just very naturally flamboyant. It wasn't something I tried to be. Like singing and breathing, it was just how God had made me. It was effortless for me to be myself and to be totally comfortable around people.

My heart was free and I didn't have a smidgen of fear in front of or around people. It wasn't something anyone taught me. I may have "caught it" from my daddy, but I believe it was how God created me. The truth is, if someone looked up the word "extrovert" in the dictionary, my picture would have been next to the word.

When I sang as a little girl, I did it to the top of my lungs and with every bit of emotion that I felt and then some. When I sang the first time in church, I was two or three years old. My first song was "When Momma Teaches Angels How to Sing."

Another favorite for us as a family was "He Looked Beyond my Fault and Saw my Need." My mother sang the verse, while my brother Doug and I had a small part as well. I harmonized on this song with my mother, dad, and brother. My dad's efforts to make us into a family fell short because he believed it could be accomplished by building it around talent.

My love of singing became a "blessing" beyond the church. There would be times that I couldn't find a quarter to buy my much needed pack of M&Ms. So I would make my way around the neighborhood and offer to sing to people for money. I learned early in life that a person's gift would make room for them and bring them before great people – the Janet Version of Proverbs 18:16. When I found an audience willing to pay me a quarter, I sang. The number one song in my repertoire was "Don't it Make my Brown Eyes Blue"!

Actually, it wasn't hard to find people who would "pay up." At a young age, I found out how to get to people's hearts; I would sing! Sharing this causes me to think that perhaps my mother felt insecure. She wasn't like me.

She was more introverted and so were my brothers. My flamboyance was a gift I shared with my daddy.

After a long time in the pantry that fateful day, thinking and crying, I made the decision to stay with my dad. My heart did not give me any other choice. I knew my daddy would fight for me! I needed a hero to protect me. After all, I was just a little girl. So I cried my eyeballs out to stay with him.

The day that my mom left me there to live with my dad was horrible. My two brothers went to live with my mom. As they walked out of the house, I felt like they were walking out of my life. My heart sank when I saw the sadness in my mother's eyes. I had chosen to stay with my daddy. But how could I leave him alone? I was Daddy's Girl.

I remember the moment of my mother's leaving the house for the last time. In my heart I can see her even now, hugging me and kissing me squarely in the mouth — that's how she would always do it — she would hold my face and kiss me on the lips. As she left, her last words to me were, "Call me if you need anything."

Aunt Sally's House

After about a week of staying with my dad, things were not going too well. I had not bathed. I had barely brushed my teeth. And worst of all, I was just so hungry.

I looked for pennies and nickels, trying to come up with a quarter to buy a pack of M&Ms. After I spent all the money I could find on M&Ms, I was still hungry. I had no choice but to call my mom. I asked her to come and get me something to eat.

It's hard to remember and maybe it's because I really don't want to, but during the relatively short time I stayed with my dad, he usually didn't come home all day long. And there were nights when he didn't come home either. When he did, he went straight to bed without eating. Since he didn't eat, I didn't either. How could I not remember that? I was so hungry!

When my mother picked me up, we went to Aunt Sally's house. I sure did love Aunt Sally. Aunt Sally was married to my dad's brother, and she was letting my mom stay there with her for a little while. That night when we got to her house, I ate three banana sandwiches! I didn't think I would ever get full! Aunt Sally gave me a glass of milk and cookies too! To this day, I love banana and mayonnaise sandwiches! People who are not from the South might be scratching their heads and wondering about a banana sandwich. Well, you'll have to try it!

After my tummy was fully tight with bananas and white bread, I took a bath! I remember how wonderful it felt to be clean. My mom had bought me some brand new PJs – at least I thought they were new – and it felt so good to be in my mother's care.

I felt secure at Aunt Sally's. For the first time, this little girl felt her mother loved her. I didn't have to do anything to earn it. It wasn't because I was a cutie. It wasn't because I could sing. It wasn't because I said the right things. It was simply because I was her little girl. She was my mother and she was going to take care of me.

In time, we moved from the warmth of Aunt Sally's home and into the housing projects. My mom was now a single working mother. And life went on.

Chapter Two

Divorce, Chaos, Confusion, Poverty

My mother was a very talented woman. She could sew and make anything. She grew up in a Christian home, or so it seemed to me from things she said. I believe she had several stepbrothers, but there was only one sibling that I remember: my mother had a sister. Aunt Sue! She was amazing! I actually kept thinking that I looked so much like my Aunt Sue! She was a very gifted seamstress too and very organized and smart! My mother's sewing abilities always reminded me of Aunt Sue.

Moving to the housing projects made me feel like we were starting over once again. And I didn't know what to do without my daddy. I missed him so very much. I don't remember seeing him that much at all in those days. There was a local church in town that knew of our family, and they knew that I could sing. I remember them asking me to come and sing at their church. I did go and sing from time to time, but it was not the same. I didn't have my daddy with me.

This church was a Spirit-filled Pentecostal Church and they were very good to us. One day I was sitting at the kitchen table, and I looked in the refrigerator only to find that there was no food. I looked in the pantry and there was no food. That was the way it often was. In fact, I had grown accustomed to being hungry. Sometimes I ate just plain bread and put sugar on it. This day, as I got ready to eat some sugar bread, I heard someone knocking on the door. It was a very sweet lady from the Pentecostal Church. She had brought some groceries.

I was so excited! There were crackers and peanut butter, Little Debbie snacks, ham and bologna, sausage and eggs and so much more. I was excited to have some food! I ate so much that day that my belly stuck out!

Growing up in the projects and being poor was no fun. Growing up without my daddy was even worse. By then, I was ten years old, and although my daddy wasn't around, there were plenty of boys in the neighborhood that *were* around. And believe it or not, the 16-year-old boys were already attracted to me and would make their way over to my house when my mom was working.

My brothers were a good bit older than I was. My oldest brother was my half-brother and he was eight years older. My middle brother was five years older. Because of that, it was natural for us to always have older boys at the house. I was always surrounded by boys. I began to find affirmation in these boys because they told me how beautiful I was and that if I were only a little bit older...

I want to take just a moment to tell some of the men who may read this book that your presence and affirmation with your daughter is vital. If you don't affirm her, then the boy next door will. If you don't spend time with her and tell her how wonderful she is, then the boy next door will. That is where the spiritual door is opened to sexual temptation. If a father affirms his daughter and has a relationship with her, it shuts the door on the temptation for her to give herself away before marriage.

There I was, unprotected and vulnerable to these guys who came to our house! I began to emotionally attach myself to these boys. There was never any sexual perversion physically, but there was a lot of it verbally. I learned a lot about sex at ten years old in the housing projects.

There were days that I begged to spend time with my mother, but she was always too tired from work. On the weekends, I noticed that she started going to the club and drinking. My Aunt Sally and her husband owned a club, so she went out with them. I stayed at my Aunt Sally's house with my cousins. The next thing that I remember after that is moving again. We finally moved out of the housing projects to a "real" home.

Brother Wayne

Our house was very small, but it was a *house* and I was so excited! Still, deep down inside, I missed my daddy. I missed seeing that guitar that he carried around with him everywhere he went just in case he needed it.

I kept thinking, *Where is my dad? Is he mad at me? Does he not love me anymore?* So many years had passed by and it seemed like I only saw him once or twice. Had I done something that made him not want to come back? Was it my fault? I wasn't singing anymore, and my daddy wasn't around.

These were very hard times in my family's life. It was still a struggle to have food. My mother wasn't home on the weekends, but we lived across the street from my Aunt Ruth. She was the sister of my daddy's mother. Ruth was a very beautiful woman. I remember that she had long red fingernails and she wore makeup and her hair was always fixed. And, more important, she always had food!

One evening my brothers and I were sitting in our house and we were so very hungry. Mom was not home, and my oldest half-brother felt the need to take care of us. I believe he went to great lengths to get us what we needed – even to the extreme that he broke into Aunt Ruth's house and stole food for us.

Stealing at this point had become a way of life for my brother. He even got into trouble at school for stealing. I kept thinking that this was wrong; but I was so hungry, it just didn't matter.

My middle brother was always really quiet, and he was very tender hearted. That left my older half-brother to step in and do what he felt needed to be done for his younger siblings. I remember him being good to me, making sure that I had all I needed. He helped me with homework and provided food, even if he had to steal it. I loved him for that.

Divorce had left me so broken and so lonely. I really felt like a grenade had gone off in my heart and left me unfixable. I wondered if I could ever recover from this.

Then Brother Wayne walked into my life. He was a children's/youth pastor at the local Assemblies of God Church. He had a bus ministry and he saw me outside one day playing in the neighborhood, so he came by to drop off a brochure that was an invitation to children's church.

I noticed that Brother Wayne had a guitar with him. When I asked him if he played, he said yes. He got his guitar out of his minivan and he began to sing and play. Immediately I started to harmonize with him. He couldn't believe it, and I loved being able to harmonize and sing again. So my mother gave him permission to come pick me up the following Sunday and take me to children's church at the Assemblies of God Church. I loved it there.

There was something special about Brother Wayne. I remember him telling me that I was a princess and that "Daddy God" loved me so much. I thought to myself, *Really? God loves me?* Brother Wayne even gave me a princess gown to help me remember what he taught me.

Brother Wayne planted the seed of God's love in me, something that I never forgot. I remembered singing with my dad and knowing how much he loved me. But I never had thought about *God* loving me like that.

The love that this man had for me was so powerful. Had Brother Wayne *not* been there at that time in my life, I don't know where I would be today. So many times as an adult, I have wanted to call him and tell him that the seed he planted in my life was not in vain. I wanted to let Brother Wayne know that I was serving the Lord and preaching the gospel and married to a pastor and it was because of him! He was just one man with a big heart for children and his vision from God to GO OUT! He alone took his bus ministry and gathered up the children. Brother Wayne showed me that he loved me enough to come by and pick me up faithfully; and because of that, my life was changed. I searched and could never find him, but I am confident that I will see him in heaven.

I want to take a moment to encourage someone who works with children. You may feel all alone, like no one is helping you, and you feel as though you are going nowhere and all your work is in vain. But through you and your love for children, you are planting seeds that will never fade away and will never disappear. The seed you plant of the love of God will grow and grow. So don't give up, even when you feel alone. Follow your vision for that bus ministry, and pray for the harvest. Pray for laborers in the kingdom to help you and serve by your side.

What you can't see is that you are changing the course of someone's life, even though you may not see the fruit of it yet. Please – I beg of you – don't quit and don't get discouraged. Today I am praying for you, the youth pastors and children's pastors, to not give up. I know it can get hard, but keep on laboring and watch, because eventually, you will see fruit. I can feel the Holy Spirit with me as I write these words to you. Don't give up and in time you will reap and see the harvest! It's God's promise to you.

Brother Wayne poured the love of God into me as a little girl. Meanwhile, my mom was still going to the bar and was drinking and dancing and doing her own thing – having a good time. Life must have been hard on her. My dad did not pay child support; we lived on food stamps. And most of the time, we lived in the projects.

My mom worked at the Van Heusen sewing factory, making the collars for men's business shirts. Momma only made minimum wage and could not support three kids on her own. I believe she went searching for someone that could help her raise three kids. Then finally, her search was over. I remember her bringing a man home with her to meet us. After only about four weeks of their being together, they got married.

Chapter Three

Remarriage, Abuse, and Abandonment

I remember this man coming to our little house. At first, he seemed to be so kind and I loved that he gave me money. I could go buy M&Ms anytime I wanted! My mother fell in love with this man, but I didn't know what to think. All I could think was, *Where is MY DADDY?* I missed him so much.

This other man tried to work his way into my heart by offering me things. He made promises to me and he always told me how beautiful I was and that he would always love me. And I thought to myself, *Is this possible*? Could this man take my daddy's place?

Then I came home from school one day and our house was packed up! It was on a Friday and we moved that weekend to a house far out in the country. It was so far away that I even had to change schools.

My stepdad's house was small but it was paid for, and he had a lot of land that he was farming. He immediately put my brothers to work on the farm, and me too. I learned how to pick corn, peas, butterbeans, okra, and other vegetables. And I learned how to feed pigs, cows, chickens and turkeys! I loved the animals. I wanted a horse so badly!

This man seemed to have won his way to my heart. I was so full of life and energy and had so much love to give and no one to give it to. He even wanted all of us to call him "daddy". This was really hard for me. I didn't want to call him daddy because he was not my daddy. I had a daddy and he was my hero; but for the moment, I didn't know where he was or what he was doing. So, even though my brothers began to call our stepdad, "daddy", I resisted. But then it grew on me and I got used to it; so eventually, I gave in and started calling him "dad".

Abuse

My stepdad told me that I was beautiful and that he loved me. He told me he would do anything for me. He even bought me new clothes. I wasn't used to this. All my clothes came from garage sales. At this point in my life, I don't ever remember getting anything new except when I was really little and my daddy put me in a beauty pageant and he bought me new clothes and a beautiful princess dress.

My stepfather took us all shopping together and I remember that he wanted to buy me panties and my first training bra. Everybody in the house made a big deal out of it. Because I was the baby and I was growing up and had started developing, it was obvious that my body was changing; but at the same time, I was embarrassed.

After a day of shopping, we would come home and I would try on all my clothes and model them for the whole family. I was so excited. But then if my mom had to leave and go to the grocery store, and my brothers left the house to go work in the fields, my stepfather would stay home with me.

After everyone was gone, he would say to me, "Go try on your panties and bra for me and let me see them." I thought this was strange and I didn't want to do it, but he promised me it was no big deal. He said that he just wanted to see what he had bought for me. I was so young and didn't understand why he wanted to see; I was innocent. So, I did as he asked. He would tell me how beautiful my body was and that he loved me. Sometimes he would even cry when he saw me.

As time went by, my stepfather began to come in the bathroom while I was taking a shower and peek in. It would scare me so badly that I would scream! He would laugh and say, "It's no big deal." Then things began to get very dark and it went from bad to worse.

Some of the things that I am about to tell you I have only mentioned a few times in my life. It is so shameful that I never want to repeat it or even talk about it. The only reason I will even put it on paper is for all the women out there that have been sexually assaulted, molested and raped as a child or as an adult.

Maybe you've been suffering with a secret for most of your life. Maybe you think that it's your fault and you've never been able to get over it. I want to share my story with you to let you know that God put me back together, and He can do it for you too.

My life went from divorce, to poverty, to abuse. I went from singing with my dad in church, to singing with Brother Wayne, to singing in the bars. At 11 years old, my mom and my stepfather took me to the bar that Aunt Sally owned and I sang "Satin sheets to lie on, satin pillow to cry on, and still I'm not happy don't you see..." I was in a country bar singing country music with a very strong twang! I saw drunks and smokers all the time and it became a way of life for me.

On the weekends at our house, there was always a party with whiskey and beer and lots of smoking. My stepfather was a mean drunk. Most of the time, he beat my brothers for no reason. And if my mom looked at him wrong, he hit her too.

I was the only one he did not hit. But it was because he was doing other things to me. It started when he told my mother that he wanted to take me to work with him. We had a lot of land where he cut down trees, so I thought that I was actually going to help him. I put on my work clothes and he watched me get undressed and dressed. It made me feel so uncomfortable.

This one time in particular, my stepfather took me to the woods in his big truck. He made me lie down in his lap and he rubbed my stomach and my arms; then he made his way up my shirt. I had NEVER been touched like that before. I didn't know *what* was happening.

My stepfather told me that he loved me while I was crying and saying to him, "Please...please don't do that."

My tears didn't stop him. He simply answered, "Relax, I'm going to make you feel good." But all I could do was cry.

Next, he moved his hand way down my pants and when he got there, I screamed, but no one could hear me because we were in the woods. Then he took my hand and made me move it down his pants. I never even knew what was inside of a man's pants, but it was the most horrible thing I had ever felt.

After he was done with me, he drove me home while I cried all the way. I said, "I'm going to tell my mom what you did."

His answer was abrupt and hard. He said, "If you tell her or anyone else, I will kill you."

This happened over and over and over again. My stepfather would always take me to work with him on Saturdays. I begged Momma to let me stay home and clean house, but she demanded that I go with him.

I was trapped and there was no way out. I can't even find the words to describe how I felt except for "dirty". I felt like trash. I felt so dead inside that I couldn't imagine how there could even be any life in me. Everything was stripped away and my life was shattered into a million pieces. I had no reason to even want to live anymore.

The weekends were always bad. When my stepfather got drunk, he became more aggressive and mean. He had never beaten me up at this point, but he did beat my mom and my brothers.

I was always afraid to go to bed at night. I knew that when I would lie down, I could expect him to come into my room in the middle of the night and wake me up by putting his hands all over me. This happened all the time. My mom wondered why I had a hard time getting up in the mornings for school.

Truthfully, school was a joke! I barely got by. But I did notice that school was my only peace. I never had to worry about food anymore, but I had lost my desire to even eat.

One day my stepfather bought a motorcycle and I saw that my brothers were riding it. I was happy for them. I had never been on a motorcycle before, so my brothers offered to take me for a ride. Then I had the bright idea that I could drive the bike myself. I was 11 years old, but they let me drive it.

After I got down the road, I tried to turn the motorcycle around to come back home. But I noticed it was really hard to maneuver. I popped a "wheelie" by accident and it threw me off and dragged me a few feet on the road. My leg was severely burned by the muffler pipe and I was torn up by the gravel on the road. I was hurt really badly, and shocked too.

A young man happened to drive by and saw me. He stopped to help. He was probably around 18 or 19 years old. By that time, I had been gone for a while so my stepfather came looking for me. When he saw me with this guy, he became really angry. He was jealous. He thought I went down there to meet this young man and then I got in a wreck. He had the story twisted in his mind and he acted on his version of what he believed happened.

I remember my stepfather putting my brother out of the car to drive the motorcycle back home and he put me in the car. He screamed at me, calling me a whore and a slut and he hit me in the face with his fists. He gave me two black eyes to go along with all the other wounds I had from the wreck.

When we arrived home, I ran to my room and crawled into my bed where I stayed for hours crying. My mother came to my room just one time to console me.

My stepfather waited until the middle of the night to enter my room. He was crying and he told me he was sorry and that he loved me so very much and he wanted to make it up to me. He began to kiss on me and touch me all over again. It was so disgusting! I hated him. But I couldn't tell anyone because I knew he would kill me.

I spent a great deal of time outside with the animals. We had a pet pig named Sally! I remember her vividly. She was my best friend, and I told her everything. She knew all that was happening to me. Because of my stepfather's threats, talking to Sally was my only outlet.

As I fed Sally her slop in the bucket, she would listen to me and do exactly what I would ask her to do. She was stubborn and would not listen to anyone except for me. I loved her so much.

One day I came home from school and I couldn't find Sally. I looked everywhere for her. The whole family knew how much I loved her. We sat down at the supper table later that evening and I noticed that Momma had cooked pork chops. As we were eating, I kept asking everyone where Sally was and they all started laughing at me.

Someone finally burst out with laughter and said, "You're eating her!" I was devastated. I jumped up from the table and ran to my room and cried my eyeballs out! She had been my best friend. No one ever told me that my stepfather was raising these animals to slaughter them! I had become attached to Sally. I loved her, and now I had eaten her. How awful! My heart still breaks when I think about that day. It was a cruel trick.

As the days went by, I became harder and harder in my spirit. My stepdad was so mean! He was evil to the core. I don't know why my mom stayed with him. The housing projects were bad, but at least it was better than this!

One time my middle brother was washing the car and he missed a spot on the wheel. My stepfather got a whip out and took him to his room and beat him until he bled. The door was locked so that no one could come in, so I banged on the door, screaming and crying on his behalf. My brother was so sweet and so kind. How could this awful man beat him like that?!

Another time, we were babysitting one of my stepfather's nephews. He was such a cute baby! He was sitting at the table with us in a regular chair because we didn't have a high chair. The baby was only about two years old, and he accidentally spilled his milk. My stepfather was so enraged over this that he took off his belt and screamed at that baby, "I told you to be still!" Then he beat that child until he had whelps all over his body. That day, something clicked in me. I was tired of seeing my brothers and my mom beaten. I was tired of all the abuse.

Meanwhile, my oldest stepbrother had completely "lost it." He had begun to meet with what he called "aliens" out in the woods. He often came back from one of his trips to tell me about all the aliens. He also became involved with Ouija boards and witchcraft. He would even hold séances outside of our house on the weekends. And through the summer, these would occur every day. I remember being in a group of people in a circle calling on the dead. It was way too weird for me. I could feel the evil and I just could not stay in it. It seemed there was demonic activity all around me.

Something Strange

One day, something very strange happened. My half-brother became very demanding of me. But by this point I was a very angry girl and I would not let him control me. I don't remember why he became mad at me; but he was so enraged that he chased me around the house with a butcher knife, threatening to kill me. Then he caught me and trapped me in a corner and held the knife to my neck. As he screamed at me, I began to pray for my very life. I was weeping and crying and begging, "Please don't kill me!"

The look in my half-brother's eyes that day was so evil that I could tell something had taken him over. But as soon as he looked in my eyes and actually heard my plea, he realized that I was his sister. He dropped the knife and begged for my forgiveness, weeping like a baby over me. That day, I stayed in that corner for hours and didn't even get up. I felt like my body weighed a ton and I could not move. And to make things worse, there was no one I could talk to.

Despite the abuse, my stepfather had a way with my brothers. My brothers gladly called him father, but my mom had to *make* me call him that. He was not my daddy; but oh, how I wanted a father to love! All I wanted was to be back in my daddy's arms again! I felt safe and secure in his arms. But at this point in my life, I was completely unprotected and vulnerable to the hands of my stepfather.

A detour

I am about to tell you story that I have only told my husband and I hope to never tell it again since I am writing this book. This is the story of my breaking point and when things changed for me and my whole family. This is the story that changed the course of my destiny and it was the best thing that ever happened to me and at the same time, the worst thing that ever happened to me.

One day I was at my house, alone with my stepfather again. Everyone had left and we lived out in the country so there were no neighbors close by. I was 11 or 12 years old. Something came over my stepfather to go a step further with me than he ever had before. In our living room, he made me take off all my clothes and he bound me to the couch. He began to kiss my whole body and to tell me how much he loved me. I cried and screamed to the top of my lungs when he made his way to my bottom with his mouth. I prayed, "God, help me!" I didn't know what else to pray or say.

Up to this point he had never tried to have sex with me, although he had touched me all over. But this day, he was going to rape me. I fought him with everything that I had. I screamed and yelled and cried and begged him to stop. I pleaded over and over, "Please don't do this. Please don't do this!"

Then something happened miraculously as he was speaking words of endearment to me. As he tried to rape me, he felt conviction and he stopped! It was as though Jesus was passing through and said to him, "STOP!" The God he did not believe in was drawn to my cry. I cried out to my God and He saved me from the plan of my enemy.

As I lay on the couch naked, tears streamed down my face. I was still yelling and wailing for someone to come and help me. Suddenly, my stepfather got up and walked away, leaving me there. God had saved me.

That night I could not sleep at all. I just wanted to die. I saw no hope for my future and I saw no reason to even live anymore. I sat in my bed and cried until my eyes were almost swollen shut. Then I remembered some pills that were in the medicine cabinet and I thought that would be a good way to end my life. So I went and got all of them and put them on my bed, resolving that this was the night I would end it all.

What happened to that little girl that used to sing with her daddy and run and jump in his arms? Where was my daddy? You know, my dad tried to come and visit me one time, but he and my stepfather got in a fist fight over me and my stepfather pulled a gun on him and told him he would kill him if he came any further. My daddy kept saying, "I just want to see my baby!" He left that day, having no idea about what was happening to me! My dad was gone and my life was over.

There simply was no more life left in me. I had been stripped of my innocence and dignity. I felt unclean and dirty! Up until that point, I had always had a way of putting things behind me, just to get through difficult times; but this was too much, and I couldn't get through it.

I decided that it was time to end my life. With tears showering my face, I picked up the pills to take them; but I paused and prayed to God right before I put them in my mouth.

Then all of the sudden, something strange happened. I heard a knock in my wall that kept moving around the room. I got out of bed and I followed the sound around the room. When I arrived at the window, I stared out through the glass and saw the moon and the stars. They were so beautiful. And as I gazed upon the beauty of God's creation, I felt a warmth come over me, like something overshadowed me. It was a presence that was so powerful that it made my heart race, and at the same time, it calmed me down and took away all my anxiety.

I heard a voice say, "Tonight, you will not take your life, but you will lie down and go to sleep; and I will show you what to do tomorrow." This voice was so powerful, and this presence was so calming, that when it came over me, I felt as though I floated to my bed and no longer did I even see the pills. I don't know where they went or what happened to them.

By the time I woke up the next morning, no one was at home. But the presence that I had known the night before was still with me. I felt as if someone was carrying me. I went to my mother's bedroom and the voice said to me, "Pick up the phone and call the police. Tell them everything that has happened." So I did. I asked them to please come get my stepfather and put him in jail because he was a very bad man. They listened and then told me that they were on the way.

Meanwhile, my mother came home and that same voice told me to tell my mother. I was so ashamed, but yet bold and fed up, and I was no longer going to live another day like the ones I had endured. I knew that it was only a matter of time before he would rape me. As I told my mother what had happened, she picked up her cigarettes and began to chain smoke and drink her beer. Then she looked at me and called me a liar.

I was devastated all over again. This was the woman that gave birth to me and the man she was married to was sexually abusing me. And she didn't believe me. I thought to myself, *Do I even have any more tears to cry?* I had already spent most of my childhood crying. I didn't think I even had another tear left. But then she looked at me and said,

"Well, if he did do this, it's your fault! It's because you're beautiful and talented and charismatic. Your body is beautiful so you made him do it. You gave him no choice."

At that moment, the wound from her words was deeper and more painful than the abuse itself. I felt as if a sword had been thrust all the way through my heart and had come out the other side. I was in shock. I felt a very heavy weight come upon me, but yet I was still determined not to back away from the truth.

Then my mother challenged me to prove it to her. It was about time for my stepfather to arrive home; so she suggested that when he got home, I should take him behind the door and see if he did anything to me. She said then she would catch him and she could see for herself with her own eyes. So I did as my mother told me to do, but all he did was hug me that day. I had no proof.

While I waited for the police to get there, I told my brothers what had happened to me, and they too called me a liar. I couldn't imagine how they could say that! This was the man that had beaten them and my mother and they still took up for him. It just didn't make sense at all.

My half-brother had become a professional liar. He could tell a lie so well that he could convince you that he was telling the truth even though you knew it was a lie! He had created a lifestyle of robbery and lying that was so natural to him that he actually convinced himself that it was all good.

No one believed me. And my own mother blamed it on me. But at the same time, I still felt very brave and courageous! I knew the police were on the way to get this evil, old man and put him in jail.

Two police cars, lights flashing, arrived in our yard. I ran out to them and told them who I was and showed them my stepfather. I remembered the gun my stepfather had when he said he was going to kill my daddy, and I feared he would use that same gun on me.

I thought that the police were going to lock up my stepfather; but instead, they took me away and left him there. It's like I was going to jail while they did nothing to him. I was so confused. He was a bad man. He needed to go to jail! The police were very kind to me and as I hung my head down in shame and embarrassment, they drove me away to another place.

That was the day it all changed for me. That voice that was speaking to me was God and the presence that I felt was the power of the Holy Spirit. I didn't know that at the time; but now looking back on it, I know that the Lord came down and rescued me. He heard my cry. He heard my prayer and He saved me from the hand of my enemy.

From that day forward, God built a hedge around me that is standing to this day. The enemy had been trying to kill me and destroy me from the get-go. But God stepped in and interrupted the schemes of the devil. He said, "I know the plans I have for you," and He reclaimed what belonged to HIM that day.

I remember talking with the counselor. She asked me to walk through all the abuse from the beginning. So I did what she asked, but with my head held down. I remember her taking her sweet hand and holding it under my chin. She lifted my head up and as I looked into her weeping eyes, she said to me, "Don't ever hold your head down. This is not your fault." I thought to myself, *Is she an angel?* I had never felt such love from a person like this.

The words the counselor said to me were the complete opposite of what my mother had said. I wondered if Momma noticed since she was sitting right beside me. Next, the lady began to counsel us and to tell us what we needed to do. She said if my mother would leave this man, she would be able to keep me.

So my mother attempted to leave my stepfather. We went to stay with my Aunt Sally again. But every day, my mom would go back and forth to cook supper for him. This lasted for about two weeks. Then it came time for the counselor to re-evaluate the situation to see how it was going.

Not knowing what was going to happen seemed worse than living with my stepfather. I didn't know that this would be the day that my life would be turned down a completely different path and that my journey would be changed so finitely. My mother had made her decision. She decided to give me up to foster care and go back to the man that abused us all.

I will never forget the day my mother left me. We were standing on a balcony of some sort that had steps that led down to the ground. It was raining outside. The counselor opened the door to the balcony to lead me down the steps to get into the car that would take me away. I held onto my mother's hands and grabbed her and begged her not to leave. I told her I would go back with her and endure whatever, just as long as I could be with her.

My mother was weeping and I was crying and screaming and begging her not to leave me. As the rain came down harder outside, it was raining even harder on the inside of my soul. Darkness surrounded me as the man picked me up and pulled me out of the arms of my mother. I screamed even louder, "Don't leave me, Momma!"

I curled up in the back seat of the car and wept as we pulled away. The counselor sobbed with me. She looked at me and said,

"Everything is going to be all right." There was such love in her voice and so much compassion that I wanted so much to believe her words. I wanted to reach out and grasp hold of hope, but I could not see where to reach.

I never saw that counselor again. Sometimes I look back on that day and wonder if she was an angel. To me, she was the nicest, most compassionate and loving person I had ever met. There was a deposit of love made that day. After so many withdrawals, I was bankrupt, but this was the day that the first new deposit was made. It was the Love of God! I was left with battle scars, but this love that I felt stayed with me. Never underestimate the power of love!

The Greatest Gift

1 Corinthians 13

Though I speak with the tongues of men and of angels, but **have not love**, I have become sounding brass or a clanging cymbal. And though I have the gift of prophecy, and understand all mysteries and all knowledge, and though I have all faith, so that I could remove mountains, but **have not love**, I am nothing. And though I bestow all my goods to feed the poor, and though I give my body to be burned, but **have not love**, it profits me nothing. Love suffers long and is kind; love does not envy; love does not parade itself, is not puffed up; does not behave rudely, does not seek its own, is not provoked, thinks no evil; does not rejoice in iniquity, but rejoices in the truth; bears all things, believes all things, hopes all things, endures all things. **Love never fails.**

LOVE NEVER FAILS! How glorious is the love of God. How wonderful He is, that He came to me through this counselor to show me real love. I remember that feeling so vividly. Even to this day, out of all the gifts that I know or have, I pursue love more than any others!

Chapter Four

Foster Care

The love I felt from the social worker was incredible and even today, I remember it. I cherish what she said to me, "This is not your fault; do not hang your head low, but look up!" But how *could* I hold my head up?!

There I was, in foster care without my daddy or my momma. I didn't ask for any of this. How could this have happened to our family?! I felt as though my whole world was caving in on me. I was under so much stress and pressure that I was severely depressed.

The first foster house I went to was the home of a little widowed lady. I think that somehow, I was kin to her. She was my daddy's great, great aunt, I believe. I can remember the smell – it was musty – and the house was cluttered. At this point, it really wasn't important who I was with because I was so angry and hurt that it turned into rebellion. I was defiant and depressed, not a good combination. In fact, I was a ticking bomb, ready to explode at any moment.

As soon as my foster mother tried to put very strict rules in place, I ran away. I packed my bags with clothes, food and water, and I ran. I didn't get very far. In just a few hours, the police found me and took me back. Then I ran away again. I was too much for this little old lady. So they took me to another foster home.

The next foster care situation was a good one, but at the same time, it was bad. It made it worse that I was confused as I tried to decipher good and bad. When people told me that they loved me, I was leery because love was twisted in my mind. After all, I was a daddy's girl and I didn't even know where he was. And I knew that he loved me, but he was nowhere around. Then my stepfather told me he loved me, but I found out that meant putting his hands all over me and threatening my life. Even my mother had confused me. She gave birth to me and said she loved me, but then she abandoned me and gave me up to foster care. She chose the abuser over me. So, what was love? I was really confused about love and what was supposed to be normal.

In this foster home, the lady was very strict. She made me clean all the time. It's because of her that I know how to clean a bathroom! But the wonderful thing about her home was that she always had Coke in the refrigerator. I thought that was awesome. We never had Coke at home. There was always a lot of beer and liquor, but never Coke.

The house was always spotless and we lived on a military base. The man was retired from the Army so we could go to the post to get food and the government also provided money to buy me clothes and to get my teeth fixed. My teeth were in such bad shape. I had so many cavities. At 12 years old, I was going to the dentist for the first time. *So this is what it is like to be taken care of*, I thought. Up until that time, I had been forced to take care of myself, and I was doing a pretty rotten job.

Finally, I had been put in a home with someone who would take care of me and would teach me to clean, cook, and be a lady. I remember this lady teaching me the very basic, simple things, like how to bathe and take care of my body, how to shave my legs and take care of my face. And I had acne! I was going through puberty and had turned into an ugly duckling! Every time I looked in the mirror, I did not see beauty, but I saw ugly! I was even confused on what beauty was. All that beauty had done for me was to make my mother hate me, my stepfather abuse me, and my father never to return for me. So, I thought I would just be ugly! That's all I could see.

A New Song

Somehow singing was still in my heart and I found I had a song to sing. I remember in the gym locker room one day, in the 6th grade, I stood up on the chair, then the table, and I began to walk on chairs and tables singing! I had the attention of the whole locker room! They all joined in singing with me. The words said, "Well, your 'Nobody' called today; she hung up when I asked her name."

I had a way of drawing a crowd to sing with me. Little did I know that all of that was training ground for becoming a Worship Leader. God has His way, doesn't He? Who can come against God? Who could snatch me out of His hand? Who could lay out a plan for me like this and take what Satan meant for harm and turn it around for my good?! Who else but the God who created the heavens and the earth and all that is in it!

It was God at work, even in darkness! It was He that was making the crooked ways straight! In all my pain and brokenness, when I would sing, people would listen. I never thought I was anything special because I was too broken to think such a thing. But music was my only escape and when I went there, I was free!

From Darkness to Light

In the foster home where I lived, there were many foster brothers and sisters. They were all wounded and abused! Abandoned and forsaken! One of the girls in particular told me about the night that both of her parents were killed. She was only 12 at the time. I remember her talking about all the blue and red lights. It was a tragic car accident. She was in the car with them, but they died and she didn't. She talked to me about how she hated Christmas because it reminded her of the red and blue lights from the wreck. She also told me about all the drugs she was doing and all the sex partners she had had. I met her when she was 16 and I was only 12. She was very broken. When my foster parents left the house, people came over to do drugs and they had orgies. My foster sister would come in and tell me all that she was doing. All the orgies, pornography, and drugs were taking me to a deeper level of sin and darkness.

One day, this girl asked me if I wanted to smoke pot with her. I said, "Sure." But I took one draw from the pot and it made me sick! I coughed until I vomited. And I never touched it again! But I remember the smell. It was distinct. Although I didn't suffer abuse from the adults in this home, there was no love; and in many ways, it was a prison to me. I was in the depth of sin and filth! I could not understand living in such a spotless house but yet feeling so very dirty! I cried myself to sleep every night, along with all the other foster kids. There were two or three of us in a room, so I could hear them cry also. Even when we slept, we cried in our sleep.

One night I was alone and I was crying. I was listening to music on the radio. Christian radio stations weren't as prominent as they are today and the signals for those stations weren't very strong. But all of a sudden, there was a loud static sound on the radio and the station changed on its own. It came to a Christian station and I remember the song that came on. It was "Rise Again". I listened carefully to the words: "Yes, I'll rise again, ain't no power on earth can keep me down. Yes, I'll rise again, death can't keep me in the ground."

That song spoke to me! It told me about Jesus. The song talked about His wounds and brokenness, and death, and how HE defeated it! I thought to myself, *I want to be like Jesus.* I knew how He felt. I was breathing and alive, but yet dead in my heart. And I knew that if I could somehow get to Jesus, He could make my heart live again.

But then I realized that I didn't know *how* to get to Jesus. I remembered Brother Wayne's church. One day I saw a bus for this church and I remembered that they had a bus ministry! They came by once again to pick me up and I went to this church, but Brother Wayne wasn't there anymore. There was a new youth pastor. I don't remember his name, but he and his family had dark skin.

Maybe they were Hispanic or Indian. But that didn't matter. I just knew that they could sing and play the guitar. This spoke to me deeply.

I remember sitting back and listening to them and just soaking in the beauty of the music. There was a sound about them that was different and I wanted it. It drew me in like a magnet. I began to join with them and sing.

Revival was breaking out in this church but for some reason, I still could not find my way to Jesus! I was searching and looking, but I could not find Him! I was in such darkness that I couldn't find *anything* or *anyone*! And I didn't think that Jesus would come into my darkness and bring light to my dark soul.

But the whole time, HE was there. I sensed Him, though I didn't know how to make Him Lord of my life. The seeds planted in my heart by this church took root in the depths of my dark, weary soul and began to grow.

The best words to describe what was happening inside me are found in scripture. The Psalmist expressed it well.

Psalm 139:7-12

Where can I go from your Spirit?

Where can I flee from your presence?

If I go up to the heavens, you are there;

if I make my bed in the depths, you are there.

If I rise on the wings of the dawn,

if I settle on the far side of the sea,

even there your hand will guide me,

your right hand will hold me fast.

If I say, "Surely the darkness will hide me

and the light become night around me,"

even the darkness will not be dark to you;

the night will shine like the day,

for darkness is as light to you.

There was nowhere that I could go that I would escape God's presence. Although I didn't ask for all this, my bed was made for me in the depths of hell. But darkness was as light to God. He is not afraid of darkness. He was not afraid of *my* darkness. David said, "Surely the darkness will hide me and the light become night around me." This was where I lived.

Even though I was in this mighty revival at church and I longed to be in this light that drew me to it, I still could not see. My soul was too dark and even the light around me became darkness.

But even in my darkness, Jesus was there and His right hand was holding me while His other hand was guiding me. The Lord Jesus never left me. God *remembered* that little girl who used to call on Him when her daddy was sick. And God *remembered* when that little girl laid her hands on her daddy's head and prayed to Jesus. He was still there with me.

All the life that was in that little girl had died, and yet God was still there. And I was learning that He would be with me, even in death. He was not afraid of my darkness and He is not afraid of your darkness either!

Jeremiah 1:5a

Now the Word of the LORD came to me saying, "**Before I formed you in the womb I knew you**, And before you were born I consecrated you; **I have appointed you** a prophet to the nations."

God said that before He formed me, He knew me. And before I was born, He consecrated me and appointed me for such a time as this.

Psalm 139:15-16

My frame was not hidden from You, When I was made in secret, And skillfully wrought in the depths of the earth; Your eyes have seen my unformed substance; And in Your book were all written The days that were ordained for me, When as yet there was not one of them....

His eyes were always upon me. Even when I couldn't be seen in my mother's womb, Jesus laid a book out in the heavens and He wrote my name on it. He was orchestrating the symphony of my life, my destiny, my song, and my journey.

Jeremiah 29:11

For I know the plans I have for you...plans to prosper you.

Not only did He know me, form me, and guide me in darkness on purpose, He set me apart and appointed me! When I think back, I can see Him at work; but at that time, all I could feel was anguish and bitterness of the soul. My spirit was crushed and my soul was wounded, making me feel as though I was all alone.

Psalm 34:18

The Lord is close to the brokenhearted and saves those who are crushed in spirit.

Even in the worst of times, God was not sleepy, nor was He tired. He was not afraid of my darkness; and in my brokenness, He came to me! God was not lost and He did not need a GPS to find me! The moment my soul cried out in anguish, He was there! I couldn't find Him, and I didn't know *how* to find Him. I went to church on occasion, and I still couldn't find Him. I was lost! And that's when the Holy Spirit became my GPS!

My Father's House

I remember the day I came home from school and my foster mother met me with a smile. She told me that my daddy had come and I was going to live with him. She said that he had been fighting for me for all those months. And he finally got custody of me and I would be moving to Tennessee! I began to cry.

I should have been happy, but I was very sad. I really wanted my mother. I wanted my *mom* to fight for me. I wanted *her* to come and get me. I told my foster mom that I couldn't go with my daddy, and that I wanted my mother instead! I was even willing to go back to the abuse if my mother would take me back.

I even found myself remembering a time when I was at the First Assemblies of God Church in Ozark, Alabama where Brother Wayne used to be. My stepdad had waited for me in the parking lot to tell me he was sorry for all the things he had done to me. He was crying and he told me he loved me and that if I would forgive him, he would make everything better and bring me back home. But I didn't know if I could trust him. Still, in my heart, I just wanted my momma! I longed for her.

In all my confusion and messed up heart, I was not capable of making a decision. My foster mother talked me into living with my dad. Since I was 12 years old, I could have made the decision with whom I wanted to live. And on that day, I went against my feelings because my emotions were all over the place and could not be trusted, and I went to live with my daddy!

In reality, I was in search for love, and I couldn't find it. It was easy for me to fall for anyone that said he or she loved me. Little did I know that it was LOVE that had created me. It was LOVE that knew me and saw me from the foundations. It was LOVE that called me and separated me. And it was LOVE that I was searching for.

God is LOVE and the world is searching for HIM and looking in all the wrong places and faces. Oh, to be a little girl again and to crawl up in the arms of my daddy where I felt safe and secure and protected! Oh, to be the apple of my daddy's eye again!

I worried how my father would see me. My innocence had been stripped from me, and my body was changing and it was shameful to me. Would my daddy look at me the same again? Would he accept me after all that I had been through? Could this relationship be restored?

I didn't feel beautiful anymore, and my song had been smothered with grief and darkness. In fact, darkness was familiar to me. Pain had now attached itself to me and I had grown accustomed to feeling it. Every day was painful. I didn't know how to deal with life if it did not offer me pain.

I suppose that going back to my mother's house was familiar and my wounded dark soul was drawn to her. But I remembered my mother saying, "It is better that you go with your father."

I recalled the moment of complete silence as I heard the sniffles from her nose and saw the tears streaming down her face. I thought to myself, *Really? You don't want me?*

I fell to my knees and cried out, "Oh God, help me!" What did I ever do that my mother would not love me?! I wanted her so badly. I loved her so deeply. I just wanted her to love me back.

All along it was HE – Jesus – who was separating me. And He led me back to my father's house.

Chapter Five

Reuniting with my Father

I packed my bags and got in the car to go meet my father. Thoughts crowded my mind as I worried about seeing him again after all this time and all that I had been through. Would he recognize me? Would he accept me? Would he love me? Would he want me? My greatest concern was that he would be able to see the filth of my soul.

I could feel anxiety rising up, and at the same time, sadness gripped me. I would be moving to Tennessee, far away from my mother! I remember opening the car door and seeing my dad standing at a distance. He was talking with someone and smiling and laughing. When he saw me, his eyes were set on me and mine on him. My heart swelled up within me as I found myself running back to the arms of my father.

I raced to him and jumped in his arms like I had always done. He caught me as I leaped like a deer and embraced him like a monkey! And he said to me, "There's daddy's baby!" He stole my heart once again with his words and his love and acceptance. What a beautiful feeling to be back with my father.

Snow and a Fresh Start

Daddy and I set off for Kingsport, Tennessee. On the drive, he began to tell me about a few things to expect. And like so many times in the past, Daddy had another woman by his side. I remember him saying, "You can just call her MOM!"

I was like, "What? You've got to be kidding me!" Not again! It was my mom who forced me to call my stepdad, "daddy" and now my dad was forcing me to call my stepmom, "Mom".

I just couldn't! I didn't even know her. I mean, "Mom" is a title you earn. You just don't call strangers MOM! And I voiced my opinion, out loud, in front of her.

She looked back at me and said, "Just call me '2 Mom!'"

Again, I was like, "What?" It was a little confusing at first.

She was an Indian woman. It looked to me that she was a full-blooded Cherokee Indian.

Her nose looked like an Indian, her eyes were very dark, and her hair was jet black and curly. She was about 4'11". She was nice, but very quiet. I have never been around quiet people like that. It kind of scared me.

But my dad was charismatic, charming, and very pleasant to be around. He always had a way to make even my stepmom laugh and smile. He was *always* cracking jokes and embarrassing my stepmother. My dad could make up a rhyme spontaneously, and it would be so funny. If he were a rapper, he would've been able to "freestyle" with no problem at all!

There were times that we went to the Waffle House and my father would flirt with the waitress, right in front of my stepmom, but he always said he was just joking. Then he and I would make up songs and rhymes, sitting right there at the table, and we both would get so loud. We would laugh out loud, for real! My stepmom would *not* be laughing, and she would always shhhhushhh us!

My dad was a free bird! He would laugh and carry on, no matter where he was. In my eyes, he always seemed to be happy. I was drawn to this. My soul had been sad for so long that it was a relief for me just to laugh and make jokes.

My stepmother explained to me how her grandkids called her "2 Mom." She said, "I'm not number 1 but I can be number 2 in your life."

She said that her grandchildren had a number 1 mom, and she was their number 2 mom. That made sense to me. I began to call her 2 Mom. *Everybody* called her 2 Mom!

This part of my life was very complicated. I was entering into my teenage years and hormones were all over the place and still my soul was deeply wounded. But things began to fall into place, even from the time that we arrived in Tennessee.

After the long drive from Alabama, we were greeted by a whole lot of people with gifts and surprises and food and a huge cookie-cake. They all celebrated *me*! I was shocked! This 2 Mom that I didn't know had gathered her whole family there to celebrate my arrival.

And for the first time in my life, I saw snow! Daddy said it was the first snow of the year. And it came when I arrived. He said that heaven was smiling on me and God sent snow to refresh me. It was so beautiful. SNOW! I didn't even have a jacket, and I lay in the snow and made a snow angel.

I was so dirty on the inside and my soul was in darkness. But I was surrounded by a host of people to greet me and God had sent me snow. And of course, my dad had the biggest pack of M&Ms I had ever seen! As I lay there in the snow, I had no other thought except for sheer delight and rest! With every breath I took, the air seemed cleaner and crisper. I inhaled and exhaled the cool air, letting it fill and refresh my lungs. It gave me such hope!

I loved the snow! It was amazing! And I loved the mountains! I had never seen mountains before. We lived in the big city of Kingsport, Tennessee. Well, it wasn't really that big, but it seemed so big in my own eyes compared to Ozark, Alabama where I grew up. And there were such bad memories in Ozark.

From that point on, the hand of God began to write a new chapter in my life. As an adult, I can look back and see that my life was a lot like Joseph's life in the book of Genesis, chapters 37-50. Joseph was loved by his father but hated by his brothers. Joseph was full of destiny but ran into quite a few obstacles as the Lord opened a door for him through rejection.

Joseph's brothers threw him into a pit and even planned to kill him. Traders came along and bought him, taking Joseph into a life of slavery. But Joseph excelled at everything he did, despite his circumstances. And he went from slavery to being second in command over all of Egypt. Joseph literally moved from a pit to slavery, to prison, to the King's palace. Each place he went was an open door from God to lead him to his destiny, a destiny that was not just for him but was for his people and their nation!

God had plans for this young man. And God had plans for me. Like Joseph, I went from a little girl in my father's house with my mother and my brothers, to divorce that led to a pit (the housing projects), that led to slavery (my stepfather's house), that led to prison (foster care). And then I was freed from my prison, and God was ready to write new chapters for my life.

Then again, sometimes I felt like the children of Israel. God brought them out of Egypt, but could he take Egypt out of *them*? Who are the children of Israel anyway? Interestingly enough, they are the descendants of Joseph – yes, the one God delivered out of the pit, from slavery, then from prison and the one who was second in command to an Egyptian king they called Pharaoh.

Joseph and his brothers and all two million of his descendants were slaves to Pharaoh! God raised up Moses to lead them out of Egypt, but they still had a slave's mentality and they had become comfortable with their bondage simply because it was familiar to them. How many times do we just settle for less, when God has so much more?

It takes change, an open mind, and willingness to follow God in order to receive His blessings – not to mention, a desire to leave a place of bondage. Fear, insecurity, intimidation, rejection, anxiety, and worry all constitute bondage. It becomes our familiar prison that we have grown accustomed to.

My prayer for you is that you will desire complete freedom from all the chains that bind you, from those things that keep you in a dark prison cell. To be free is to love again, to live again, and to be YOU in all your glory and splendor!

At the ripe age of 12, I was ready to leave "Egypt". But Egypt was not ready to let go of me!

A Song Again

I was in my father's house. My dad was so proud of me. He took pictures of me and carried them in his wallet and in his Bible. Everywhere Daddy went, he took those pictures out and he showed everyone. He put me in every beauty pageant and talent show that he could find. He had me singing everywhere.

These were the days we would sit down at the kitchen table and my dad would play his guitar and sing and I would harmonize with him. It was just Daddy and me. My stepmom couldn't sing. But I remember that she loved to hear *us* sing. Everybody did!

Everywhere we went, my dad carried his guitar and we sang. Daddy was passionate about music. To the extreme! When he woke me up for school every morning, he brought his guitar and sang me out of bed! I was like, "Daddy, *please!*"

I remember pulling the covers over my head and begging for him to shut up! But he would just laugh! I look back on that now and wish I could only hear my father sing over me again while I was asleep. What comfort it brings me now to know that my heavenly father sings and rejoices over me today!

Zephaniah 3:17

The Lord your God in your midst, The Mighty One, will save; He will rejoice over you with gladness, He will quiet you with His love, He will rejoice over you with singing."

The Lord my God is with me, He is mighty to save, and with gladness, He rejoices over me and settles my troubled soul with HIS love.

And God sings! I wondered if God plays the guitar too!

God's Guitar Lesson

After Daddy died, I felt empty, like my dad was stripped away from me. By this time, I was a worship leader, preacher, teacher, singer/musician, and Spanish facilitator at church. I was also a hairdresser, mother, wife and whatever else I needed to be! In fact, I had three jobs. I was doing hair one day a week, working in the church six days a week, and traveling and speaking at conferences. I was writing songs and singing them and had hopes of making a CD.

After my daddy died, it all came to a halt! I still carried on, but the inside of me stopped. In chapters to come, I want to walk you through how God led me to complete the healing of abuse, abandonment, and rejection in my life. But first, I want to tell you how I know that God plays the guitar!

It had been three years of my journey of healing since my dad had died. I missed him terribly. Daddy left me his black guitar, but I didn't know how to play it. My dad had tried to teach me when I was a child, but it was too painful to wrap my fingers around the neck of that great big guitar when I was a little girl. My small hands just didn't fit. So, after my father's death, I bought a guitar stand and put his guitar in the corner of my room.

I saw that guitar every day and it reminded me of my dad. One day I was grieving over him and my loss – not just the loss of my father or my mother, but the loss of my life and my childhood.

I was angry! I was angry that I was grieving alone. I was angry with my husband, I was angry with my in-laws, I was angry with my church, I was even angry with God. Perhaps these were the darkest times of my life. It even felt worse than all that I came out of.

It was a very dark time for me, and yet my soul still searched for love and healing. One morning I woke up longing to hear my father sing, and I looked over at his guitar. Then something supernatural happened.

I felt Jesus walk into the room. And let me tell you, it was a dark room. The sun was shining outside, but it was dark on the inside of that room. I felt the Lord sit down beside me, like he had done many times before, and he said to me, "Pick up your father's guitar and today I will help you play. I will teach you."

I felt His Spirit enter me as my feet touched the cold floor, and I made my way over to my daddy's guitar. I even felt the hand of the Lord help me pick it up. Though I had never played before, I started strumming through the tender guidance of the Holy Spirit. I could already play the piano, so the Lord compared it to piano and taught me. I had no other teacher – just God.

Within two weeks of that day, I played my first song in church on the guitar. The song was called, "Standing" by William McDowell and Martha Munizzi. The words "we will face the darkness around us...break the chains that have bound us...and see the supernatural" were my story. What a perfect song for the Lord to show me as my first song on the guitar.

I know for sure that God knows how to play the guitar and the piano. That day, in my own darkness, when I felt like I was drowning in my grief and loss, Jesus came to me with such love and did the supernatural. At 41 years old, I picked up the guitar for the first time and played. The Holy Spirit showed me the song and He taught that song to me.

But little did I know that I was already doing the supernatural. This was NOT a show, my worship was real, and it was in my spirit. As I grabbed my guitar for the first time on a Sunday morning, I greeted the congregation with a huge smile on my face and told them what the Lord had done. Unashamed and unafraid, I picked up my daddy's guitar and played something I had never played before. And these were the words: "We will see what we're waiting for, the supernatural!"

I have never really been shy; but I did go through a very insecure season in my life, trying to find out who I was and what my purpose was. I felt like there was always something big on the inside, but on the outside, it was war. And whenever the battle waged too strong, I would just simply retreat.

My father and I were reunited when I was twelve years old. And I stayed in my father's house until the day I got married at the age of 19. I spent seven years with my father. Seven is the number of completeness and perfection (both physical and spiritual). It derives much of its meaning from being tied directly to God's creation of all things.

I didn't realize the meaning of this until now. God knew all the details of my life, down to the number of my days.

Chapter Six

Looking for Love

At 12 years old, I was wounded and broken. Free from Egypt but still with Egypt in me. Imagine being in middle school, broken, and wounded, insecure and stripped of all innocence. Middle school is tough when everything is normal, yet alone when a person is wounded and broken.

I was the new girl, everybody was talking about me, and I had to try to find where I was going to fit in. Music was always the way for me and I was very athletic also. I began to take acrobatics and became a cheerleader. I used my gifts and talents to win people over. I worked very hard at my cheerleading. It was a sport to me and I was serious about it.

Winning Ways

I went to two different middle schools and three different high schools! Throughout my years in school, I went to 11 different schools all together. I was always the new girl. I always had to try to win people over. So I covered up all my hurt and ignored it, and I acted as though it did not even exist. I had some people really love me, while others really hated me. Some people who *said* they loved me to my face just hated me behind my back. I never knew whom I could trust.

But I had made a way for myself. I was trained to perform in order for people to accept me. I was trained that if I looked a certain way, people would love me. I was trained that if I gave things to people, they would be my friends.

So, for me, relationships were built on my talent and abilities, my looks, and how much I could give. And all the time, I was in search of love and acceptance. I was trying to find my way. Trying to find peace in my life. Trying to escape from my internal Egypt.

Issues

I remember one day my daddy telling me that I would grow up and fall in love, and that I would leave him for my Prince Charming. That statement always made me feel so sad because the word "leave" sounded too much like "abandon" to me! I had been abandoned and I never wanted to make anyone else feel abandoned.

Abandonment had been an issue with me for a long time. I felt I had to work really hard at keeping friends and making them love me, just because I didn't want to be rejected and abandoned again. I was rooted in rejection. Even up to my early 40's, I found myself running around trying to win people's approval – especially that of my family – by constantly serving.

I don't like the word "no". To me, "no" meant, "I don't want you, I don't like you, and you are worthless." So, to avoid hearing NO's in my life, I just wouldn't ask for help. Needless to say, anyone who offered to help me became my best friend, for "helps" was my love language.

My dad was always willing to help me. I remember telling my father that I would never leave him. I would marry, but we all could live together! That makes me really laugh now.

Being a teenage girl raised by her father wasn't easy. But it made me pretty tough. I learned all kinds of things from my father. He made me feel independent and he taught me to rely on myself and not on others.

Even so, I felt empty inside. I was on a journey, looking for love and friendship. But the friendships I built were always planted on a rocky foundation because they had conditions. I knew that a faulty foundation could only lead to a tumbling house, but I wasn't sure how to fix that.

Chapter Seven

Finding Christ, Finding my Groom

Finally the day came when someone invited me to church. We had moved again and this girl was my new neighbor. She was a cheerleader at school. Because of the timing of our move, I missed try-outs and this would be the only year I did not cheer. It was devastating. How would people know who I was? How would I connect with people? But at least, after eleven different schools, this would be the school I would graduate from.

I remember thinking that cheerleaders in Georgia did things differently than what I had been taught in other states. In this particular school, gymnastics didn't play that much into being chosen as a cheerleader. Even so, I felt a real kinship with my cheerleading neighbor Alicia and she became my best friend.

Alicia's sister invited me to come with Alicia to a Sunday night revival. We decided to go! One invitation changed everything.

I later found out that the moment I walked into the sanctuary, my future husband, Cary, who was leading worship, noticed me. He said that he felt the Holy Spirit tell him that I would be his wife, the one he had been praying for. It was good that I didn't know that at the time, because I wasn't interested. I had five guys pursuing me, my heart was broken and tired, and I didn't even want to date, much less engage in a serious relationship.

The evangelist was full of fire as he spoke. He preached hard. In fact, he called Alicia and me out and said, "You two girls have been laughing and this is serious work!" It was a little unsettling to be pointed out like that, but my heart was drawn to the altar anyway.

Nothing could stop what God was going to do in me. I can't tell you one word that was preached, but the worship and the singing pulled me to the altar. I knew this was the night that the Holy Spirit would heal me.

I gave my broken heart to Jesus. I was saved and baptized in the Holy Spirit. Immediately, I began to sing at the altar. What God did that night was overwhelming. My future groom was staring at me, listening to the Holy Spirit tell him that I was to be his wife, but I was staring at God, saying, "Fix me."

Answered Prayers

God answered Cary's prayers for a wife – someone who was Spirit-filled, someone who was musical and could sing, and someone attractive that he was drawn to – and God was also answering my prayer to fill the emptiness I had lived with for so many years.

After that night, Cary invented ways to pursue me. Since I worked at Wal-Mart, Cary came to shop there. He stopped me and said, "Don't I know you from somewhere?" fully aware that I was the girl he had seen at church.

I looked back at him, and our eyes connected. I answered coyly, "Well, I don't know," thinking to myself how cute he was.

Cary said, "I think you came to my church. I was leading worship and I saw you." At that moment, I felt myself being drawn to him. My palms got sweaty and my heart beat fast. Just his presence made me melt. Looking back, I think it was the Spirit of God on him.

At that time, there were several guys pursuing me, showing signs of interest by leaving flowers and notes, calling to schedule dates, and showering me with attention. But Cary was different. He stood out separate from the crowd.

Cary had heard how strict my daddy was and how hard it was to get his permission to date me, so he cleverly invited both Daddy and me to sing at church. My dad and I went to the Church of God on Saturday to practice and sing for Cary.

We stayed about two hours and then Cary and I sang "He is More Wonderful" together. A different style of music was introduced to me that day, more contemporary than the blue grass Southern gospel my dad sang. Daddy fell asleep on the front row, so it gave Cary and me time to bond.

After a while, it was nearing lunchtime. Cary again invited my dad and me to sing at church and then slipped in that he wanted to take me to lunch. Although Daddy was usually adverse to anybody taking his little girl on a date, Cary was musical, so it softened Daddy's heart and he said yes.

That lunch became the first date of many, and we fell in love immediately. It was really strong. There was so much energy between the two of us! We were engaged after six months.

A Surprise

I'll never forget the 4th of July, 1988. We had been talking about getting married, but I never thought it would come about so quickly. Cary was six years older than I was and he was ready to have a wife. He waited for me to graduate from high school.

Then on the 4th of July, he took me to Savannah. On River Street, he pulled a ring from his pocket and asked me, "Janet, will you marry me?" Everything inside of me was exploding. Only my skin held me together.

I jumped and shouted, "Yes, yes, yes!" Maybe it surprised him that I hugged him in public since his family is more private; but I didn't care – I was excited – and I came from a long line of huggers! This day, my emotions were transparent. I was overjoyed.

As time went on, the energy between us was challenged. As our relationship grew, it became a tug of war between my future husband and my father. Since Daddy was a "church hopper," he didn't understand my new allegiance to God and this church. Up until that time, my service had been to my father. Whatever my daddy scheduled me for – beauty pageants, talent shows, programs in which I sang – I always went and did what he asked.

But Cary saw deep into me and found there was so much more than a singing talent. He became my mentor and taught me the ways of the Lord. In my heart, I had already walked away from my father's house and had become connected to Cary, something that my father didn't understand or like. He didn't understand that I couldn't go places with him on a whim because I was committed to a church that served God. He never stopped me from going, but I could tell he didn't like it.

No Holding Back

I had such an encounter with God; I was sold out to Him one hundred and ten percent. My dad was a good man and had taken care of me; but everything I had searched for my whole life was in the power of God that I continually saw demonstrated in this church. It felt like the power of the Holy Spirit was healing my heart and I was drawn to stay there. It was the only thing that filled the void. I recognized it because I had been searching so long to find it.

Those things I couldn't find in cheerleading, singing, or even in my father's house, I had found here. There was no turning back. It wasn't that I didn't love my father; but I couldn't stay away from God's house.

I even remembered the cheerleader from High School who is a Christian recording artist and wondered how she could have kept this Jesus to herself. *If this is what she was experiencing,* I thought, *how could she have held this back?*

During this period of time, I attended Cosmetology School to become a hairdresser. But that wasn't my focus. It was my profession and I loved doing it, but what lived inside of me was more than that. I knew that I had to let people know what Jesus could do for them. I didn't even have to *try* to witness. It just bubbled over out of me.

I had made up my mind that I was not holding back what I had. I quickly became a preacher, though I never knew I was called to be one. I shouted the Gospel from the top of my being. I sang. I witnessed. I walked with Jesus.

It was more than just going to church. I had a *relationship* with Him. I felt His presence. I longed for the Word. I was always praying. And I had a good teacher – my husband respected me and taught me the ways of the Lord from the first days we were together.

Courtship

Cary treated me so differently than how I'd ever been treated before. Even before we were married, Cary's walk with the Lord protected our relationship. He never said, "If you love me, you will sleep with me." He never even saw me in a bathing suit until we were married.

Cary loved who I was on the inside. And that made me love him even more. Looking back, I believe that's the glue that held us together. We never jumped ahead. Those dating days supplied the foundation for our relationship. The Holy Spirit of God kept us.

We decided to wait until there was a vow and a commitment to give ourselves to one another physically. And we were careful to never give the enemy a foothold – we didn't spend time alone, snuggling or kissing, until we were married. It wasn't easy, but we guarded our hearts.

Abandonment was still an issue for me. There were times Cary took me home from church and when he started to leave, I cried and said, "Will you come back?" Because of what I had been through, I was afraid he would leave me. Always before, those people who said they loved me had left. Nothing had ever turned out good for me. I was afraid that this was too good to be true and would never last.

Once we were engaged, I felt compelled to tell Cary about my past. I just knew that when I told him, he would leave me and I braced myself for that. But as I was laying out all that I had lived through before my husband-to-be, I noticed he was crying. He said powerful words to me: "I love you and I'm never going to leave you. I love you even more now."

Those words – *I'll never leave you* – were words I'd never heard before. The bond was so powerful. It was electrifying. At that point, even in Cary's words to me as my future husband, I felt God saying it as well, "I'll never leave you." This was the first step of my healing journey.

On our wedding day, I sang "Our Love in Christ Will Be All Right." I chose this song because Christ was the center of our relationship and I knew if God said it was okay, then that was a promise. My emotions said Cary would leave me because everyone else had, but I knew to stand firm on the Word of God.

And sure enough, Cary kept showing up. He kept on loving me. Through Cary, the Lord was teaching me that Jesus loved me even more than Cary and that He would never leave me. That's what made Cary such a good mentor. His heart has always been like that. Even today, after 25 years of marriage, he is kind and forgiving. I still see it.

We got married August 19, 1989 after having been engaged for a year. I wanted to start having children right away.

Chapter Eight

Heart's Desire and Heart's Loss

Right from the first of our marriage, we began to plan our family. I didn't know that the journey ahead of me would be long. I had no idea of the trials I would face in the next few years.

All I had ever longed for my whole life was to have a family of my own. My dreams and my desires were to be a mother. I didn't ask God to give me anything else – not wealth, fame, or a big house – none of the material things of life, not even a big career. All I asked Him for was to be a mother. It was my one heart's desire. Now that I was with this man that was incredible, I wanted to have his children.

It didn't bother me that after three months, I wasn't pregnant, because I knew it was early in our endeavor. But after six months, I began to think that something was wrong. I went to see the doctor and I had laparoscopic surgery. Afterward, he told me that I had polycystic ovarian syndrome. What this meant was that even though I had a cycle, no eggs were released and my ovaries were enlarged.

We started infertility treatments, but still nothing happened. A year passed. I was grieved in my heart. The disappointment was beyond what words could even say or describe.

I was devastated. It was to the point that whenever I saw a pregnant woman at Wal-Mart or any other place, I cried. I was consumed with trying so hard to have a baby that my insides were stiff.

A Promise

I remember one night when we were in revival. The Lord must have been looking down on me, seeing far in advance and knowing what was ahead. Yet, He looked at my grief for that moment and gave me a word.

The evangelist stopped his sermon and called me out of the congregation. He said, "You've been seeking God for something and you need an answer. Within seven days, you'll have that answer." By the time I got home, I was beginning to feel nauseous. I thought for sure that I was coming down with the flu.

Within seven days – just as the evangelist had said – I was pregnant with my first child. And everyone soon knew I was pregnant! I've never been a private person. My husband's dad was our pastor and almost the entire congregation had heard the prophecy. They were rejoicing with us.

Everyone at the hair salon where I worked also knew. They brought me balloons and cake. The celebrations had gone on for weeks. I was ecstatic...but it only lasted for a short while because I miscarried at three months.

I was very sad and I cried a lot. But it gave me hope that I had been able to get pregnant. I believed that if I could get pregnant once, it could happen again. Every month for a year, I took a pregnancy test. I wasn't discouraged. I just *knew* it would happen.

But after a year and twelve negative pregnancy tests, I started infertility treatments again. This was the third year of our marriage, the third year of trying to have children.

Meanwhile, in this process between our second and third year, Cary and I were experiencing a hard time in our marriage. Because of my wounded past, I still feared he would leave me, especially if I couldn't give him children. Once again, my husband proved his love. He was loyal and faithful. He told me, "You, Janet, are my heart's desire. And if you never have children, I am okay with that. I want you. You're enough for me."

Failure

Yet, there was emptiness in me and a sense of failure that I couldn't give my husband children. I almost felt as if God had rejected me and that maybe He was punishing me. I wondered if I wasn't good enough to be a mother.

I remember crying so hard that I became ill and vomited. Sometimes I wept so much that Cary would pick me up off the floor and carry me to my bed. He put a washcloth over my face and prayed over me. He always saw something more in me than I could see in myself.

I remember that when Cary prayed over me, he called forth the prophetic and musical gifts that were inside of me. It was as if he could already see that I would be a preacher and a songwriter, though I was so blinded by my grief that I never saw it. The miscarriage and loss of that child was bad enough; but now after two years of no results, I was beyond grieving. I felt hopeless.

Christmas was a particularly bad time of year for me. I dreamed that Cary died. I had finally believed that he wasn't going to leave me; but yet, I still didn't believe anything good could happen to me. This was evidenced in my dreams where I believed I was at his funeral, and I woke up crying.

The enemy was tormenting me, but I was such a young Christian that I didn't know how to fight back. I didn't know that in Christ Jesus, He blesses us and prospers us in our journey. He requires that we have faith to believe in the impossible. But at that time, all I felt was hopelessness. Satan kept telling me over and over that Cary was going to die.

Answers

One day, my Daddy God stepped in and said, "Enough is enough." I had begun a journey of prayer and reading the Bible. I was simply reading the Ten Commandments and I got to the part where it said that if you honor your father and your mother, your days will be long and satisfied.

A light went off in my soul and in my head, and all the darkness that was there couldn't stay. Truth was the light, and it set me free from the grief and the enemy who was trying to kill and steal my husband away from me. The Lord said to me, "Has Cary not loved and honored his parents like no one you have ever seen?"

I heard God's voice so clearly; His voice was so powerful, loving, and kind. In an instant, it wiped away my fear of losing my husband. I trusted in that Scripture. I knew that Cary had loved and honored his parents and that he would live a very long life. I never had that nightmare again. When it left, that fear was gone completely and it never came back. Scripture says, "The perfect love of God casts out all fear."

Our journey to have a baby went on for five years. During this time, I remembered a pair of baby booties that my friend's mother had crocheted for me with my first pregnancy. They were pretty little white booties with a blue string in them. I pulled them out of the closet.

I had read the scripture where it said that if you delight yourself in the Lord, He will give you the desires of your heart. I thought that maybe God wanted me to adopt. I knew that I had always wanted to feel my baby in me; but if that wasn't God's will, I was okay with it. I had finally reached the point that I was okay if it didn't happen that way. So I put the booties by my bed and I set adoption papers there also. Every night for a year, I prayed over those booties and over those adoption papers. Still, nothing happened.

Hannah

Near the end of that year, I started fasting for peace. I had already been praying. I read the story of Hannah, a woman whose womb was closed. Hannah prayed at Shiloh and she grieved so much that the priest thought she was drunk. She fell over on the ground. I thought to myself that it sounded just like me. Then the Lord spoke to Hannah and said that He would give her a child *in time.*

The story is found in I Samuel 1:1-20:

"Now there was a certain man...and his name was Elkanah...And he had two wives: the name of one was Hannah, and the name of the other Peninnah. Peninnah had children, but Hannah had no children.

This man went up from his city yearly to worship and sacrifice to the LORD of hosts in Shiloh. Also the two sons of Eli, Hophni and Phinehas, the priests of the LORD, were there. And whenever the time came for Elkanah to make an offering, he would give portions to Peninnah his wife and to all her sons and daughters. But to Hannah he would give a double portion, for he loved Hannah, although the LORD had closed her womb. And her rival also provoked her severely, to make her miserable, because the LORD had closed her womb. So it was, year by year, when she went up to the house of the LORD, that she provoked her; therefore she wept and did not eat.

Then Elkanah her husband said to her, 'Hannah, why do you weep? Why do you not eat? And why is your heart grieved? Am I not better to you than ten sons?'

So Hannah arose after they had finished eating and drinking in Shiloh. Now Eli the priest was sitting on the seat by the doorpost of the tabernacle of the LORD. And she was in bitterness of soul, and prayed to the LORD and wept in anguish. Then she made a vow and said, 'O LORD of hosts, if You will indeed look on the affliction of Your maidservant and remember me, and not forget Your maidservant, but will give Your maidservant a male child, then I will give him to the LORD all the days of his life, and no razor shall come upon his head.'

And it happened, as she continued praying before the LORD, that Eli watched her mouth. Now Hannah spoke in her heart; only her lips moved, but her voice was not heard. Therefore Eli thought she was drunk. So Eli said to her, 'How long will you be drunk? Put your wine away from you!'

But Hannah answered and said, 'No, my lord, I am a woman of sorrowful spirit. I have drunk neither wine nor intoxicating drink, but have poured out my soul before the LORD. Do not consider your maidservant a wicked woman, for out of the abundance of my complaint and grief I have spoken until now.'

Then Eli answered and said, 'Go in peace, and the God of Israel grant your petition which you have asked of him.'

And she said, 'Let your maidservant find favor in your sight.' So the woman went her way and ate, and her face was no longer sad.

Then they rose early in the morning and worshiped before the LORD, and returned and came to their house at Ramah. And Elkanah knew Hannah his wife, and the LORD remembered her. So it came to pass in the process of time that Hannah conceived and bore a son, and called his name Samuel, saying, 'Because I have asked for him from the LORD.'"

The verse that said "it came to pass *in the process of time* that Hannah conceived" particularly spoke to me. I felt like Hannah. This passage marks the first place in the Bible for fasting and prayer together. Hannah had set the example because of her grief over not having a child.

For a week after that, I prayed for complete peace. I knew that God understood that I wanted a child, so I didn't even pray for that. I needed for the grief and the torture to stop, so I just prayed for peace.

I only ate bread once a day and drank nothing but water for a week. On the seventh day, when I finished my fast, I got up from my knees and was filled with peace. I wasn't worried anymore. I was happy. I still kept the baby booties and the adoption papers by my bed, and I knew that God would provide and He would make a way.

I remember the Lord waking me up in the middle of the night and saying, "Tonight, you will conceive." I was still learning the voice of the Lord, so I wondered, *Is this God or is this me?*

Nevertheless, I woke up Cary and said to him, "Baby, the Lord says we will conceive. Tonight's your night." My husband was very happy.

Within seven days of that night, I heard that voice again. This time, there were details of what was happening in my body. The Lord told me that the sperm and the egg had united and they were in my fallopian tube. On the seventh day, He told me the promise had been implanted in my uterus. God assured me that it would stay.

It was almost funny yet doubtful at the same time. This voice was unique. The message was detailed – and since I'm not a "detail person," I knew it wasn't from my brain and couldn't be overlooked. It was God.

Within two weeks of conception, I heard the Lord say, "Take your temperature. I'm going to show you when the hormone level goes up." I had learned in fertility instructions to take my temperature and that it should spike in the second week and stay up. Never before had my temperature stayed up. It had been 95.6 in the past but now it was 98.1.

For me, that was off the chart! And it stayed there, just like God said it would.

I remember the morning I got up to brush my teeth and I almost threw up in the sink. Up until that point, I hadn't told anyone about the voice I had been listening to. When I was a week late for my period, I still didn't think anything too much about it except that I was slightly nauseous and incredibly hungry. It was, in fact, the deepest hunger pain I had ever experienced in my life.

I never took a pregnancy test. I had done that so many times in the past with negative results, that I didn't want to be disappointed again. I was still learning to hear God's voice and I knew that His voice never disappoints. I knew it would be different this time. There was something new going on inside of me.

The day that Cary and his mother took me to Savannah to buy a car, I was so hungry that I was ill with them for taking so long at the car dealership to make the decision about the car. The time for lunch passed and we didn't get to eat until well after 5:00. When we finally sat down to eat, I turned green and couldn't eat a bite. All the way home, I moaned and groaned. Then the voice came to me and said, "You're pregnant."

I woke up the next morning to go to work at the hair salon. I was in the process of opening my own business, my own salon. I remembered the scripture Isaiah 30:21 where God promises to be a voice. "Whether you turn to the right or to the left, your ears will hear a voice behind you saying, 'this is the way, walk in it.'"

And that's just the way it happened. I heard the voice behind me, giving me instructions about conception and opening my own business, all at the same time. Still, I wasn't 100% sure it was HIS voice. On this day, I gave my two-week notice, knowing I had six weeks to get a new salon ready.

Around noon that day, I thought that I would get a pregnancy test and take it when I went home to eat lunch. My husband and my mother-in-law were at home because they had a cleaning business together. I went upstairs to take the pregnancy test in secret. I didn't even let Cary know. Cary's mother was on the first floor, but Cary had stepped out. When the pregnancy test showed a positive result, I screamed. I jumped up and down and did a back flip.

I ran down the stairs and thought, *How am I going to keep these emotions inside of me? I really need to tell Cary first but he's not here!* A million thoughts ran through my head. I thought of so many ways to tell Cary. Should I wrap up the pregnancy test and put it in a box? Instead, I called him on the phone, standing in the stairwell.

Since I had screamed, my mother-in-law came running, worried that something was wrong. When Cary answered the phone, I didn't even say, "Hello, baby." I just screamed, "I'm pregnant, I'm pregnant" over and over. I must have said it a hundred times, screaming and crying.

My mother-in-law rejoiced with me and then joked, "That explains why you're eating so much!" Cary came home and we all celebrated together.

Within a week, I became ill. I vomited all day long like someone with a stomach virus, except that it didn't go away for six months! I threw up every day, sick and opening a new business at the same time. It was one of the hardest things I've ever done. Twenty-four years old and with so much on my plate! But when the nausea left, I ate.

At six months, you might hardly have known I was pregnant because I had only gained ten pounds. But after the nausea passed, I found that food was amazing. *Everything* was good, those banana sandwiches with mayonnaise! I could eat six in one setting. Forty pounds later, I gave birth to my first child, all natural. It was an incredible experience.

I never laid that baby down without being right beside him. I held him all the time, feeling him close to me. His very breath was a promise. I knew Reed was my little Samuel. I spoke over his whole life, asking God for Reed to be like Samuel, a man that would know God's voice.

Within a few months of giving birth to my first son, I was ready to try again for a second child. Two years passed and nothing happened, so I thought maybe I should try the "bootie thing" again. I fasted for a week and put the booties by my bed. Within three months, I was pregnant with my second child.

It never dawned on me to change the blue strings in the booties. God knew every detail and I was having a boy. But we were having the hardest time naming him. About two weeks before he was born, I sat down at the table with my friends and family and I felt the name drop out of the sky, like rain falling from heaven. I knew it was the Lord. He said, "His name will be Rhett McKenzie Swanson." I didn't know what that name meant until after he was born. I looked it up and found that it means "shepherd". I named him Rhett, but the Lord named him Shepherd.

After eight hours of labor, Rhett entered the world via C-section. When I brought him home from the hospital, Reed fell in love with his brother, slept with him, petted him, and cared for him. I heard the Lord say "Pray for their love. It will be special. Always teach them to love one another because their bond will be strong." I brought them up, praying three things: that they would always love God, always love their parents, and always love each other." And they have always been very close.

Cary and I became closer to the Lord going through a discipleship class based on the book and workbook *Experiencing God* by Henry Blackaby. This study was the beginning of a new chapter in our life together. During that year and especially through the summer of 1999, we heard the Lord tell us that something new was ahead. We felt the tugging of the Holy Spirit through the story of Abraham when he felt the Lord telling him to leave his father's house and go to a place that God would show him.

The same voice that spoke to me before about the conception and names of my children was the same voice that said, "Sell everything you have and follow me." Cary and I both had businesses – the cleaning business and the hair salon – and we were doing very well financially. I kept having dreams that I was jumping out of an airplane with no parachute. I'm not afraid of airplanes, but I would never skydive. It is my number one fear above all things to fall out of an airplane. No wonder my fears were manifested in that kind of a dream!

In my dream, Cary, Reed, Rhett, and I were jumping from a plane with other people from the church. God made it so plain and so clear, but it was still hard. Imagine selling everything that you had! I think God was showing me that taking a step of faith is stepping out into the unknown and that the initial step is scary. And in my dream, I never totally fell. I always woke up. I realized that faith meant jumping even though I saw no landing spot and there was nothing holding me up at the time of the jump.

In the middle of these reoccurring parachute dreams, I had a dream that I was at the salon working. I was so tired in my dream. My legs hurt badly. I could feel my body aching all over. But I just had one more client to do. It was late. I turned around and didn't see my client in my chair anymore. Instead, there was a large tall man sitting in my chair. His shoulders were at least 80 inches wide and thick. And he had to be at least nine feet tall because even sitting in the chair, he still soared way above my head.

His hair was long and thick and the most beautiful shade of blond that I had ever seen. I was captivated by the color of his hair. As a color specialist, I knew this shade of blond was unique. I had never seen it before. It was perfect. I knew that there was no way I could humanly achieve this color.

Then all of the sudden, he grabbed my hand and stood up. Once we were standing next to one another, he began to speak. I will never forget his voice. I remember the moment he grabbed my hand, and I felt love poured out on me. He held me with one hand. Then he held the other arm straight out in front of him, showing me a golden path with lots of light. I saw ditches and alleys and gutters, but yet flowers and gold and beauty. There were workers dressed in orange lined up alongside the path that I walked with this heavenly being. I knew he had to be my angel.

He said to me, "The Lord has sent me to you to show you what is ahead and to let you know that He will never leave you nor forsake you all the days of your life. He has sent me to protect you and guard you and show you the path ahead. The road is long and lonely and hard, but I will be with you wherever you go. I will never leave you."

Probably every time the angel said a sentence, he included the words, "I will never leave you." Maybe he said that because I feared that people *would* leave me. The Lord calmed my fears by sending an angel to be with me all the days of my life, an angel who would never leave me.

The angel spoke again, "You're going to make it and you're going to do well. Even though it's going to be hard and you'll want to give up, you won't, because I'm here." Again he said, "I will never leave you." At that moment, I felt love like I had never felt before and I was overwhelmed with warmth.

The angel picked me up and carried me because I was so tired. Then we appeared in my room and he laid me on my bed where my husband was lying. The angel bent down and kissed me on my cheek like a daddy would do when he tucked in his little girl at night and pulled the covers over her as he secured a kiss on her cheek. So I felt my Daddy God do that for me. I had been kissed by my Father.

I immediately woke up, still feeling His presence in the room. Healing came to every part of my body. From the top of my head to the soles of my feet, I felt it rush through. I had had an encounter with God my Father. At this point, there was no other option but to sell all we had and to follow Him to the place He would show us.

God said to sell our businesses, so we did. We had a beautiful home. But God said to sell our home. Nobody had ever come to us before, wanting to buy either business or our house. But God said to do it. So we followed His leading and He sent buyers without even the first bit of advertising. The people came to us, asking to buy our businesses and our house.

October 1st, 1994 was the first day my salon opened for business. Five years to the day, I signed papers to sell it. The number five is significant to God as a number of offering. It is also associated with grace, Levitical offerings, and by Jesus multiplying the five loaves of bread into a bounty that was enough to feed thousands. I felt like that was so significant because our businesses were given to God. We gave up all the income we were making and gave it to the Lord as an offering. He spoke to us, "You haven't given up houses or land that I would not give back to you in this lifetime."

Rhett was two and Reed was four when we moved to Griffin, Georgia where Cary became the Music Pastor at Harvest Temple. He was the Moses and I was the Aaron. My husband couldn't read music or play an instrument, but I was in the background and did everything for him so that he could stand before the people and lead them. It made me happy. It was beautiful because I was truly my husband's helpmate.

It never had dawned on me that I would be a pastor's wife. Little did I know that there was more to come. Just as God prepared David on the backside of the desert to be a king, He was preparing me behind the scenes to be a worship leader and I didn't even know it.

The Lord had a plan that included me the whole time. God came to me in many dreams, in a season of intercession where I felt God's presence strongly. I had dreams of my mother and stepfather in the bed, with me in between. I literally saw hell pulling my stepfather by his feet. But I was paralyzed in the dream and couldn't move. Neither could my mother. This dream occurred often. It was horrible. The presence of that hell that I felt was the worse feeling I had ever experienced. It made me feel sorry for him and pray for him. I didn't want him to go to this horrible place called hell.

A few months after that dream, my mother called me and told me that my stepfather had experienced a heart attack and died. Even though I had witnessed to him and forgiven him, he never acknowledged that there was a God or that Jesus was the Son of God. He only acknowledged a "higher power" and good and evil. He never acknowledged God as his Savior. It grieves my heart because I tried to tell him, as did my aunt. What I felt in my dream was horror in the face of hell, and I didn't want anyone to go there.

The day after my stepfather died, my mother called me, weeping and crying and begging me to forgive her. I said to her, "Mother, I forgave you a long time ago. I love you and I forgive you."

She said, "I know now that you were telling the truth. Today, nine of your cousins came and sat down at the table and told me all the horrible things that your stepfather did to them – all the sexual abuse – and how their lives had been scarred."

The truth was finally revealed after 18 years had passed. The truth finally came out. God showed me that day that He always reveals truth – always. And God showed me that vengeance was His, that my job was to forgive and that He would take care of the oppressor. It was a monumental moment for me. They always said I was a liar. That day, God vindicated me. Shortly after that, my mother became very ill. I went to see her often as her health declined.

Meanwhile, I had a very strong desire to have a third child. Four years had passed since Rhett was born. I put the booties by my bed again, fasted for a week, and I prayed the same scripture that if I delighted myself in God, He would give me the desires of my heart. God's timing is perfect. He dreams bigger than we could ever dream for ourselves. Within three months, I was pregnant.

I shared my joy with my mother although I'm not sure how much she really understood since she was so sick. During this time, she gave her heart to the Lord. My aunt and uncle led her to the Lord as I lay at her feet and wept. My aunt took the ring from my mother's finger and gave it to me. Knowing how strong a woman of God she was, I felt like she did this under the unction of the Holy Spirit so that I could have a reminder that signified my mother's love for me.

I asked my mother to move in with me so that I could take care of her, but she said no. She refused to leave the place where she had lived her whole life. I had two children to take care of and we were in full-time ministry; so when my mother seemed to rally, I went home. One morning, I woke up and felt the Lord telling me that my mother was dying.

I was in Griffin, Georgia, and my mother was in Alabama. We talked every Saturday morning, and when I didn't hear from her, I knew something was wrong. I told Cary, "My mother is dying. I can feel her leaving me."

I picked up the phone and dialed my mother. My half-brother answered the phone and said, "She can't talk. She's asleep."

I answered, "Can you just put the phone to her ear and let me talk to her?" I spoke to her but she was only able to moan and acknowledge that she heard me.

When my half-brother picked up the phone again, I asked, "Is she moving? Is she breathing?"

He said, "Yes, I put her in her bed." I thought that was strange since my mother always slept on the couch due to her osteoporosis.

I got a phone call around 4:00 that afternoon from my half-brother that my mother couldn't talk and he thought she wasn't breathing. He called 911 and the paramedics came. This call was followed by a phone call from the coroner. He questioned me about my half-brother. He said that "things" didn't look right in her bedroom. She had torn skin and handprints on her arms where it looked like someone had shaken her. The lamp was knocked over and the phone was on the floor.

The coroner questioned if my brother had "helped" my mother that day, that perhaps she was passing already and my half-brother helped her on the way out of this life. It was horrible.

My half-brother was angry that he was being questioned. He was a good liar and I believe he was possessed by many demons. There were reports that my half-brother had tried to commit suicide and was out of his head. But a person deep within him loved our mother, so I didn't know what to believe. Maybe a demon in him suggested that if he killed her, she wouldn't suffer. The autopsy did show many broken bones.

I left Griffin that day and made a seven-hour drive to join my family. Since my daddy lived right down the road, I stayed at his house. I was four months pregnant by this time.

Although my mother left me nothing, I had to pay for her funeral and make the arrangements. I remembered a song by Dottie Rambo called "He Looked Beyond my Fault and Saw my Need." I couldn't think of a better song that epitomized my mother's life. I sang that song at the service, knowing that she was secure in His arms of love. I knew my mother was in heaven.

My mother was the most kind and tenderhearted person you could ever meet. And from my neck down, I look just like her, though I favor my father in my face. After I buried my mother, I grieved so hard. I had those same feelings of abandonment flood over me once again. I thought, *How could she leave me when I am pregnant?* Momma had never been with me when I was pregnant before and I felt this had been her last chance.

To add to my feelings of abandonment, I had to deal with the fact that my mother didn't leave me anything – not a chest of drawers, or pictures – nothing of sentiment or any remembrance of our life together. I felt like it was nothing to her. She left everything to my brother and my half-brother. One brother was in prison for murder and the other one was possessed, a homosexual, and sometimes out of his mind. He was however proven innocent of hastening my mother's death.

One day in particular, I was grieving the loss of my mother and feeling overwhelmed with the abandonment that I felt because she didn't leave me anything. The Lord came to me again. Just His voice calmed my anxiety and He said to me, "You have not sold houses or land that I will not give back to you. I am your Father and I have an inheritance for you." That was enough for me. I had dreams after that of my mother in heaven. In my dreams, she kissed me and I knew everything was okay. I was at peace.

I gave birth to Ryan in February, two weeks before my birthday, and a few hours before Valentine's Day. I had supernatural childbirth. God was in it all. Six women were in the room with me. The nurse had to be an angel, full of the Spirit of God. Just as the Holy Spirit fell in the day of Pentecost, the same thing happened at Ryan's birth. The moment he left my body, every woman in the room was weeping and crying and speaking in tongues, even the nurse. I felt the heavens open up and I knew that my mother was finally there for the birth of my child, peeking over the balconies of heaven. I felt her presence.

The spirit of God flooded that place to the point that another nurse in the room said, "I have been a nurse and delivered babies for 30 years and I have never felt what I felt in this room today. I don't know what it is that you have, but I want it." She gave her heart to the Lord that day. From the moment of his birth, I believed that Ryan would lead many people to the Lord and that the presence and power of his birth ushered in the first soul of his ministry. All the angels were rejoicing.

The power of the Holy Spirit fell in that room that day. Ryan's name means "Little King." The Lord told me he would be like Gideon. The Bible says that Gideon was the "least" of his brothers but was the greatest at the end. The Lord told me that he would be a "sustainer" in our old age.

I knew that the Lord had given me a special gift for what had been taken away.

Chapter Nine

Season of Loss

After Ryan was born, I became severely depressed. I had never been depressed to that degree before. I felt as though I was walking under a huge dark cloud. I had just lost my mother, and then there were the changes of hormones from having a baby paired with no sleep. It was almost more than I could handle. I remember feeling guilty about everything.

The enemy was really tormenting my mind again. He kept telling me I was ugly and that my husband Cary didn't want me. He whispered that I was a bad mother, wife, and daughter. He kept telling me that it was my fault that my mother died. I believed that I had put her through so much grief from my abuse that the grief had killed her.

But this voice had a familiar tone to it. I had heard it before. The enemy even went so far as to play back past events in my mind, reminding me of the words that my mother said to me after I told her about my abuse. "It's your fault," she had said, "because you're so beautiful and talented. You made him do this to you!" And so this voice that had become so familiar drummed into me this thought over and over again: "Everything is your fault."

A False Burden

I carried a false burden that did not belong to me. But I didn't know how to get rid of it. By this time, I was preaching and teaching discipleship and still supporting my husband in the music ministry. But I was grieving. I didn't know anything about inner healing at that time.

Little by little, God was healing me by pulling out all the "junk from the trunk." God was in charge of my heart and my life. I had already given Him permission the day I gave Him my broken heart. It was by His mercy and compassion that He allowed things to surface so I could be set free.

But I had no idea how painful healing could be. In order to get free, I had to let God enter into the dark places of my heart. Little did I know that the words my mother spoke over me would haunt me my whole life. I found myself working for people's approval.

I worked for my husband's approval, my children, my pastor, my friends, and even for God's approval. I didn't want things to be my fault, so I worked hard to be perfect so that I would be accepted and loved.

After my mother died, it was really hard to get rid of the emotion that accompanied this deep feeling of guilt. It even made me sick. Then one day, while reading the Word of God, I came across a scripture that challenged the believer to put on the garment of praise for the spirit of heaviness.

I had always been a worshiper. But even in prayer and worship, I would weep. I was so tired of crying. I wanted to be in God's presence and worship Him, and I didn't want to cry anymore. I heard His voice say to me, "There is joy in My presence."

Truly the Joy of the Lord became my strength. I began to *pursue* joy. I read about how to handle grief and how to shake off depression. I chose my thoughts. In other words, I *chose* not to think about certain things. I became free from depression and heaviness and I felt the Lord walking with me. But even then, I still had an open wound of false burden bearing that came from deep down inside me.

Moving Again

The season came for our family to move from Griffin. We felt God calling us back home to Statesboro to help Cary's father in ministry. Ryan was barely 2 years old, Rhett was almost 8, and Reed was 10. Cary was going to be the Care Pastor at his father's church.

We had made the decision to move back and meanwhile, the music pastor had resigned from the church. They asked me to become the new Worship Leader. I couldn't believe it. I wasn't even sure I could do it. I didn't even know how, really.

I had no formal training. All I knew for sure was that I could sing, teach harmony, and play piano. I could read music or make up a part to sing. I grew up in a musical family. We always were singing and harmonizing. And I heard the Lord say to me, "Give ME what you have and I will increase you." I didn't know what all that meant, but at that moment the Lord Himself became my teacher on how to lead worship.

We moved back to Statesboro in 2006. I started working one day a week at the same salon that I sold. I worked 4 days a week at the church. This was my dream! – to be a minister of music and to lead people into the presence of God. Sometimes I feel like it was the reason I was created. I was created to worship. I was created to sing. I was created to lead. I was so excited! But I didn't know all the demons of envy and jealousy that I would have to fight off in order to live my dream.

Quickly, people became jealous and talked about me. I believe it was because when I worshiped, I didn't hold back anything. I was so in love with Jesus that I gave Him 110% of everything I was and had. I was sold out!

Singing came so very natural for me; but leading was something the Lord had to teach me. I could lead people to His presence, but leading people to unity was more difficult for me. I just assumed that everyone was like me when they got saved. And I thought that everyone talked to God and prayed and depended on HIM. I never looked to a minister for healing or comfort. I always looked to God. Perhaps this was because my father-in-law, Wayne Swanson, and Tommy Powell from Griffin, Georgia were the only pastors I ever had.

My father-in-law taught people to depend on God and to look to God for everything. He never allowed people to put him on a pedestal, although the people he pastored honored him greatly. And Tommy Powell was a preaching power house! He always relied on the power of the Holy Spirit to operate in his ministry. He was a man full of compassion and love for the people. He and his wife were very good to us and treated us like friends. They always led us to God's presence. But leading people to unity was new to me.

The Lord began to show me how to become a mentor by preferring my brothers and sisters. The Lord taught me to see the gifts that He had placed within them and to stir them up. I provoked people to become all that God had meant for them to become.

Little by little, the jealousy subsided and I won the hearts of the people. Life was good! Church was good! Worship was good! Preaching was good! Work was good! Everything was good!

I wasn't quite sure how to handle "mountain top" experiences – you know, when everything is going well. I was so used to being in the valley that being on the mountaintop was a little uncomfortable. So, with a still and reassuring voice, the Lord spoke words of comfort when I felt restless.

A Closed Door

I didn't realize it, but God was starting something in me that was going to hurt badly. God was about to reach deep into my heart where there was a door in the very back, unopened, and covered with cobwebs. This door was off limits to everyone. But it was the reason I had struggled with guilt and inadequacy.

The Lord was about to show me that I had idols in my life. I had set up "words of affirmation" from people as an idol. If things were not just right, I felt like I had to fix them. I was in a mode of striving to be accepted.

I was a hard worker. I was a mother of three boys, part-time hairdresser, Worship Pastor, wife, and serving on the music board of the Church of God, traveling and ministering at conferences, and heavily involved with missions. Learning to speak Spanish was one of my strongest priorities. I spent a lot of time with my Mexican friends, and I picked up the language pretty quickly. But I was so busy being busy! I was a worshiper, but I had idols in my life.

Then I came across this scripture and it shook me. In Revelation 2:4, I found the letter to the Church in Ephesus:

"These are the words of him who holds the seven stars in his right hand and walks among the seven golden lampstands. Know your deeds, your hard work and your perseverance. I know that you cannot tolerate wicked people, that you have tested those who claim to be apostles but are not, and have found them false. You have persevered and have endured hardships for my name, and have not grown weary.

Yet I hold this against you: You have forsaken the love you had at first. Consider how far you have fallen! Repent and do the things you did at first.

If you do not repent, I will come to you and remove your lampstand from its place. But you have this in your favor: You hate the practices of the Nicolaitans, which I also hate.

Whoever has ears, let them hear what the Spirit says to the church, To the one who is victorious, I will give the right to eat from the tree of life, which is in the paradise of God."

I knew I had become this kind of person, but I didn't know how to be different. So, in response to this scripture, I began a season of prayer and asked God to change my heart and to teach me His ways – to create in me a clean heart.

Back to my Father

It wasn't long after that, the Lord spoke to me and said, "Go to your father's house for Thanksgiving because this will be your last

Thanksgiving with him before I take him with Me."

I told my husband what the Lord had said, and he said that it would be impossible for us to go because my dog was pregnant and we could not leave her. But I told my husband that I had to go. I knew what I had heard was from the Lord.

I left my three children, my husband, and my dog two days before Thanksgiving in order to obey the voice of the Lord and to be with my father. I went back to my father's house.

First, I honored my father by cleaning his house. It was a mess. And I cleaned it so that it was spotless. Then I went to the grocery store to stock up on groceries for him and to prepare for Thanksgiving.

I cooked my father a big Thanksgiving dinner. We had his brothers and nephews over and I rejoiced with my father as we spent what I knew would be our last Thanksgiving together. Then I traveled home that evening.

My dog was waiting for me. When I arrived, she was outside the house. She would walk a bit, then lie down, then she would walk, then lie down and moan. I told my husband that she was in labor. He said she had been doing that all day. But she waited until I got home to have her puppies and I was right there to help deliver her babies. God already knew the day the puppies would be born, and He knew I wanted to be with her.

Almost a year later, on October 27, 2008, I called my father. I didn't know this would be the last time I would hear his voice. My middle brother was released from prison after 17 years and got to spend that whole year with our father.

My father spoke with me that day with such joy and laughter. He told me how much he loved me and that I would always be "daddy's little girl". He said he could not talk much that day because he was struggling with breathing, and I could hear him wheezing over the phone. But our conversation was good. I had no idea he was so sick because he was so happy and joyful. I couldn't tell that he was dying.

When we got off the phone, I heard that same voice saying, "Your father will not be here much longer." That whole day on October 27th, I asked for people to pray. I told my children to pray. I asked the church to pray. I asked my husband to pray. I knew it was time. I called him back several times but my brother would always say that Daddy was unavailable. He was either in the shower or asleep.

At 6:00 that night, I called back again and my brother said that Daddy was in the bed sleeping. I asked my brother to go in the room to see if he was breathing. When he walked into the room, I could hear my father snoring. So I thought that perhaps I was just imagining things. But I couldn't quite shake the feeling that something was about to happen.

The next morning, I woke up to take my boys to school. I was already weeping for my father. I took Rhett to school and I asked him to pray because I still had a feeling that something was wrong.

When I got home, I entered into my prayer

closet of intercession, staying with the Lord until around 9:00 a.m. Then I went to shower and to get ready for the day.

I was still at home by myself when I got a phone call from my brother, just a little after 10 o'clock. My brother was crying and he said, "I think Daddy is dead."

And I was like, "You *think?*" What was he trying to say?! I was screaming at my brother to check him again.

The coroner got on the phone and said to me in a gentle voice, "Sweetheart, your daddy is gone!"

I said to him, "Are you sure? Can you please check him again? Go back and check him again!" With tears shooting out from my eyes and grief filling my heart, I felt as though someone had punched me in the stomach and knocked the breath out of me. The coroner told me again how sorry he was, but that my precious daddy had taken his last breath around 6:00 a.m. that morning. That is about the time I started grieving for him.

All the emotions flooding through my soul were overwhelming. I jumped in my car and drove to the church where my husband, my in-laws, and the whole staff were working. I opened the back door to the church and I screamed at the top of my lungs, "Cary, Daddy is dead! My daddy is dead!"

My husband came running out of his office, and the staff came quickly out of their offices too. Then I saw my in-laws come into the hall and I fell to my knees weeping. I kept repeating over and over, "My daddy is dead, my daddy is dead! Now I have no one. I am an orphan, and I am alone!"

As I groaned and moaned in my grief, the whole staff hovered over me weeping, crying, and praying for me. The day I fell to my knees in that hall, every emotion of pain, abandonment, abuse, disappointment and guilt flooded my heart all at the same time. It was more painful than I can even describe. Remember the door that I told you I had closed in my heart that God wanted to heal? God went there that day, and He opened it.

Grief had flooded my soul to the point I could

not even walk. My husband picked up my limp body, carried me to the car, and drove me home. Our Children's Pastor, Julie, went with me to the house and packed my children's clothes while I packed my own bags to go to Alabama.

I was Daddy's little girl. I had always been close by my daddy's side. We went fishing together, we swam together, we sang together! And I was going to have to bury my father.

When I first saw him lying in the casket, I felt as though a part of me was in the coffin with him. I was raised by my father. My dad had been there in high school when my heart was broken by a boy for the very first time. He was there through my cheerleading days! He was there at the birth of all my children, he was at their birthday parties, he was at my graduation, and he was at my wedding. He was always there for me, and now he was gone.

Daddy had believed in me more than anyone else besides my husband. My heart was breaking. Daddy was gone, and there I was, on October 31, 2008, putting my father in the ground.

Within a decade, I lost both my mother and father. I was 33 when I lost my mother and 38 years old when my daddy died. I was an orphan.

My Turning Heart

The drive home was really hard. My eyes were swollen and chapped from crying. And the moment we made it home from my daddy's funeral, we received a phone call. Cary's brother was in the hospital because he had experienced a heart attack. No one knew if he was going to live.

My husband was so tired, but I looked at him and said, "You'd better go; you don't want to have any regrets." So Cary got up and left me to go to the hospital.

My brother-in-law was in the hospital for a month. They lost him on three separate occasions, but he came back each time. During that time, the church rallied around my in-laws and my husband, but no one saw my grief. I was truly alone.

I had one friend who stayed by my side, but even she could not reach me. All the state officials in our denomination recognized my father-in-law's grief. They showed up for him. The church continued to lift them up. Cards came flooding in for them when I had received only two. I was at the bottom of their list. So I thought.

It seemed like everyone supported and prayed for my in-laws, but everyone soon forgot about my loss. I just kept going. I kept preaching, teaching, and leading worship.

On the inside, my heart was turning from everyone, even from my husband. I felt that I was no longer his priority. Our marriage began to suffer and my heart grew cold.

Chapter Ten

Healing at Last

In the days that followed, it seemed as though everyone had forgotten what had happened to me. The church and Cary's side of the family became so busy that they focused their attention elsewhere, leaving me to grieve alone.

I didn't realize that this was all in God's plan because this was the final stage of the healing from my past life. I learned that the past has not "passed" until you are healed from it.

There were things that I had put behind that one hidden door of my heart that were not healed. And I had closed that door tightly so that no one could open it. Then God went there.

He began inner healing – and it was painful. But if you really want to be healed, you have to let God go into your most private place and touch the one thing that hurts the most. My deepest wound was that of abandonment.

It had scarred my life, even more than the abuse itself.

This man that I had fallen in love with was now focused in other areas of his own life and I didn't feel I was his focus. Always in the past, I had captured his attention in his every moment. He adored me. And now I felt like this was gone.

It took a while, but I eventually realized that it wasn't him – it was me. God was working on my abandonment issues and my fear of Cary leaving me. Because of this, my heart actually turned away from my husband. In fact, my heart turned from everyone...except God.

God's Breath

Our marriage suffered. My children suffered. I cried every night, weeping for my father. Still I was by my husband's side in church and in the hospital, ministering to people. But then I always went home and cried myself to sleep. I remember one time in particular that I was in prayer and I sat down at the piano to sing a personal song of worship to the Lord. God showed up beside me. I felt His very breath, flowing on me.

I felt His hand go deep and He touched me on the inside of my heart. It was so powerful that it knocked me off my chair and onto the floor. The Lord ministered mightily and yet tenderly to me. I realized that He had been there all the time. As I spent precious hours with the Lord that night, I remembered the dream I had when the angel walked beside me. He had told me that hard times were ahead but that He would never leave me.

Transition

The season of my personal healing actually came during the transition of my father-in-law handing down the mantel of Senior Pastor to his son, my husband Cary. We loved everybody in the church and we thought everyone loved us. The day that my husband became the Senior Pastor of the church was one of the hardest days of my life because this was the day that people's hearts toward us were revealed.

But God was in it all. He knew that if I could stand through this, I could stand through anything and then my heart would be forever healed of abandonment.

I had always been afraid of people abandoning me because I loved deeply and sincerely. So I believed if people told me that they loved me, they really meant it and that they would stay with me through the good and the bad. But I had a very rude awakening.

For a year – every day – we got a phone call or a letter that broke our hearts. They were not nice letters. They were letters of condemnation and accusations of inadequacies, telling us why we were not qualified to be senior pastors. Mainly they felt we were just too young. Cary was 45 years old, but many felt he was too young to be a senior pastor.

A lot of people resented me because I didn't look like a pastor's wife. I asked the Lord, "What does a pastor's wife look like?"

I felt like proverbial stones were being thrown at me as people criticized the way that I looked. They accused me of being too flamboyant, and one person even said I was too "sexy." I thought, *Where is that coming from? That is ridiculous.* No one cared how I looked when I was the Worship Leader. But when my husband became the Senior Pastor, I was "too much to handle."

Every day – and I'm not exaggerating – *every* day, we read these types of letters from church members who were not happy about the transition. We held each other and cried and prayed together. We felt like there were those who wished they could push us out.

One of our mentors that we loved and cared about began to tell people that if they would stop paying their tithes, we would leave. People actually did that. Our income was cut and we bled out – spiritually, emotionally, and even financially.

On top of that, this was the period of time that our middle son was diagnosed with Crohn's disease. He became very sick and was hospitalized on and off for over a year, to the point that we had to take him out of school and enroll him in a homebound program. My oldest son began to suffer with peer pressure and the youngest son began to harden his heart as he fought for attention.

It was a difficult time and there was no doubt that Satan was attacking our home. It was a season of tears.

During the first year of being senior pastors, it was all we could do just to keep our heads above water. Church members were leaving right and left. The second year, my husband started working hard to gain the approval of people, trying to grow the church and "clean up" the mess that was left from the dissenters who eventually left. But this was the season that God showed me things in my heart that I didn't know were there.

My heart turned from my husband and his heart turned from mine. Our marriage suffered so much that I didn't even want to be around Cary. It was cold as a graveyard in our home, but no one knew. I was so angry with him – I felt like he was married to the church and it was more important to him than what was happening in our home.

But almost every Sunday, Cary got up and declared that Satan would not have our marriage. He even declared it before the church because he knew my heart was hard toward him. I didn't know how God was ever going to put us back together. I was so broken.

My issues with abandonment were fueled by those church members who had left. Then they talked about us in the community. And yet my husband was always at church, never at home with me. I felt like he left the marriage and I wasn't number one anymore because the church was. He didn't even look at me the same way he had. I did everything to capture his attention; and when it just didn't happen, my heart became hard.

Every night, I heard a voice say, "Your husband doesn't love you anymore, and he's going to leave you. The church is more important, and you're not. He just wants you by his side to look good."

That voice was so strong. And I was so hurt and so vulnerable that I believed that lie for more than a year. I really didn't think Cary cared about me or what was going on with me. I was still grieving – my father and my mother were both gone and I had nobody but him – but the church had him and I was angry. I don't know how I led worship that year, except that angels carried me through by the grace of God.

Demons

One weekend, I decided that I would leave and go to Atlanta to spend time with my friend. I just had to get away. It was right around Christmas and we had a tradition of getting together that time of year, so my trip didn't have to be explained. I didn't tell her anything about the situation at home. It was a deep dark secret.

I stayed the whole weekend. She and I went to the mall and went shopping. We were having a good time; but then something strange happened one night at the mall. We were tired because we had shopped all day long. We sat down on a lounge chair, facing each other, our feet propped up.

We were laughing; and all of the sudden, two older men approached us. They seemed to be in their seventies and had accents like they were from Israel. As soon as they came up, one of the men began to talk. I knew it was the voice of a demon. In fact, I recognized that it was the same voice that for a year had told me that my husband didn't love me.

The man actually sat down beside me and put his arm around me. Then he said, "I know why you're here. You're running from your husband. He doesn't pay you enough attention anymore. As a matter of fact, he doesn't even love you. He puts his work first. You're running from everything. You've tried everything you could to get his attention and you can't even turn his head. So now you've run to this place. You're running." He finished his speech by laughing at me.

What the man said to me made my friend angry. She rose up and said, "You'd better get your hands off her. She is a woman called by God and you will not touch her."

He got up and said, "Oh, I'm from the Holy Land. I'm from Israel. I know about God things." Then he laughed one last time and walked off.

I just sat there and thought, *What was that?* His presence had been evil and demonic. My friend was caught off guard because she had no idea what was going on at home. At that point, something clicked inside of me. I thought to myself, *The enemy speaks no truth. He always speaks lies. And I have believed a lie for a year.*

Shortly after that, I went to the grocery store and I saw a woman staring at me. It was eerie, in that she appeared at the corner of every aisle I went down. Each time that I turned, there she was, waiting for me. Finally, on the last aisle, I walked past her and she started chanting. I could tell she was a sorceress.

She chanted, "Woman, you are so powerful. I can feel power in you when you walk by. Come to me and I will tell you your future. It is powerful."

I knew she was a witch and it sent cold chills all the way down my spine. I had just had an encounter with a demon at the mall, and then this! I knew this wasn't normal.

This was warfare. Satan was trying to take me out – kill my marriage, kill my children, and kill me.

A Return to my Love and a Revelation

I came back that weekend, rejoicing because I knew the truth. I knew whatever was said to me by satanic forces was indeed the opposite of the truth, and that my husband did love me.

I'll never forget the night I came home. I couldn't wait to see Cary. I ran into the bedroom where he was lying down. And we stayed up and talked for hours. I told him what had happened. We cried together and we laughed together. One moment, we'd be crying and the next we were laughing. Healing began to take place in my heart.

The Lord revealed the unforgiving spirit and anger that I had been holding inside and He brought to the surface everything that was behind that closed door.

Then God attended to me in my sinful state. He dealt with those demons. I didn't have to do anything but surrender and believe the truth. God did the rest.

Truth

The moment I began to believe the truth about me, my husband, and my family was the time that things turned around and went in a totally different direction. We had almost lost everything. Our medical bills had skyrocketed. We were already in debt from our income being cut, and then my second son became so ill. But then there was a break-through. God began to change it all.

The Lord showed me something through a friend of mine – my pianist – who went through surgery for a perforated colon he had from a car wreck. I stayed by his side and took care of him while he was sick. At the hospital, they had to cut him from mid-chest to his naval, and they wouldn't sew him back up. I asked the nurse why and she said they *had* to leave the wound open.

Her answer resonated in my soul and God spoke to me through her words. "A wound that is very deep has to heal from the inside out," she explained. "If you sew it up, it will leave a hole and gangrene will set in."

At that point, the Lord spoke to me and made me understand that when we have hurts so deep that we put a mask on as if they are not there, it leaves a hole in our heart, and that's where gangrenes of bitterness and anger begin to grow. It will kill you if you don't let God take care of it.

Although my friend was the patient, the Lord showed me through this man that my wounds were as deep spiritually as his were physically, and that my healing wouldn't happen overnight. I would be sore for a while, but in time, I would be healed completely. I became God's patient, and He took care of me and stood by me in the same manner that I was standing by our pianist.

I have a scar. And with deep wounds, the scar doesn't go away; but I don't remember the pain anymore. In the Bible, Joseph said that God enabled him to forget his pain.

I had held all the hurt from all of those years in my heart. Then God cut me open into the deepest of places. He allowed the storms of our church and my marriage to bring to the surface every infected area – holes in my heart that were holding gangrene and that were killing me on the inside. He opened the wound and He cleaned it out. Then He left it open so that I could heal from the inside out.

Restoration

God says in His Word that He will restore everything that the cankerworm has stolen. (Joel 2:25) Everything that had been lost, God replaced.

Our church has tripled in size since those first members left. Our marriage is stronger than ever before. My son is almost in remission and I know God is going to heal him. My oldest son is studying to be a minister and my youngest son is strong in the Lord as well. All three of my children are serving God. I stand with a scar, but whole – no holes in my heart – healed by the Almighty Physician, Counselor, and Prince of Peace who put all the broken pieces back together.

If God did it for me, He can do it for you. Allow Him to go into those places of your heart that you hide – all the holes that life has left you with. Let God open you up and let Him heal you.

I stand more humble than ever before. There is not one ounce of pride in me – God knocked it all out during that trial. And I'm okay if people don't like me. Honestly, it's okay. It's a nice surprise when they stay. And I'm okay with that. All criticism goes to God. And all compliments go to God because it all belongs to Him anyway.

In the book of Jeremiah, God says that He will heal you of all your wounds and He will rebuild you. God is my builder. It's not me. I'm not building anything. I'm amazed to see what He does and how He brings people into my life and how He is building His church.

The Lord continues to lay stone upon stone. My future – my life – is all His. It's in His hands. I know that storms will come and go in my life, but now my past is my past because I am finally healed.

Janet Swanson's Bio

Janet Swanson is Worship Pastor at the CrossRoads Community Church where her husband, Cary is the Senior Pastor. Janet and Cary have been married since 1989 and have three sons (Reed, Rhett & Ryan). Her family is her total devotion and is her greatest passion. **Janet** has been faithfully in ministry since 1988. She is an ordained minister.

Janet sings, leads worship and composes music and drama. Her piano skills and musical talents are recognized by ministry leaders who entrust her to serve on boards, to direct praise and worship in conferences and leadership meetings.

Spanish and Spanish-speaking people are dear to **Janet's** heart. She has dedicated much time and effort to achieve fluency in Spanish. She is called to translate in local schools and hospitals. She has a missionary heart and uses it regularly to share the Gospel.

Janet is a fervent preacher and teacher of the Word of God. She is called upon frequently to lead praise and worship seminars. She is a popular speaker at women's conferences in and beyond her denomination.

Her ministry as Worship Pastor at CrossRoads Community Church is a priority with **Janet**. Personal time with the Lord is the single most influential factor in the success and significance of **Janet's** life and ministry. Her greatest satisfaction in ministry is when she is leading people into God's presence for salvation, healing and deliverance. Janet has a strong prophetic anointing which is especially manifested as she ministers in music. She values every opportunity to advance the Kingdom of God and is ready to do so any place, any time.

Contact Janet Swanson at
CrossRoads Community Church
23923 Hwy 80 East
Statesboro, Ga. 30458
Janita370@yahoo.com
www.janetswansonministries.com
912-764-4539

My Mom & Dad

My Dad's
GED Ceremony

1988 My
Graduation

My Family

Engagement

My Three Sons